*Seeing America
and Its Great Men*
THE JOURNAL AND LETTERS OF
COUNT FRANCESCO DAL VERME
1783–1784

Count Francesco dal Verme. (Courtesy of Count Gian Carlo dal Verme)

SEEING AMERICA AND ITS GREAT MEN

The Journal and Letters of Count Francesco dal Verme 1783-1784

TRANSLATED AND EDITED BY
Elizabeth Cometti

THE UNIVERSITY PRESS
OF VIRGINIA
CHARLOTTESVILLE

THE UNIVERSITY PRESS OF VIRGINIA
Copyright © 1969 by the Rector and Visitors
of the University of Virginia

First published 1969

Standard Book Number: 8139-0255-x
Library of Congress Catalog Card Number: 69-17333
Printed in the United States of America

Acknowledgments

I am profoundly grateful to the descendants of Count Francesco dal Verme of Milan for having made available to me his journals and letters from abroad. I especially wish to thank Count Luigi dal Verme and Count Gian Carlo dal Verme, the former for his preliminary investigation of the Francesco dal Verme Papers in the Dal Verme Archives and for his contribution of biographical material, the latter for his assistance during the microfilming of the above papers and for his numerous kindnesses during the preparation of the present work. I am particularly grateful to Count Gian Carlo dal Verme for his critical reading of the sketch of Count Francesco and for providing photographs and genealogical information. Without the gracious interest of this distinguished Milanese family, the present account of post-Revolutionary America could not have been presented.

I am greatly indebted to George Carbone and Cesare Laviola for their help in translating the Dal Verme Papers and to Anita C. Hutcherson for her able assistance in editing them. My indebtedness for specialized help and information also extends to the following persons: Marie-Annick Blanc, Archives de la Martinique; Rema Falconer, West India Reference Library, Jamaica; Walter B. Greenwood and Mary F. Loughlin, Division of Naval History, Department of the Navy; F. M. Hutson, Archivist of South Carolina; H. G. Jones, Archivist of North Carolina; Marchesa Elisa Cornaggia Medici; Vernon Nelson, Archivist of the Moravian Church; Mary T. Quinn, Assistant for Archives of Rhode Island; and Murphy D. Smith, Assistant Librarian, American Philosophical Society.

I wish to thank the Yale University Library for permission to publish the text of the letter of President Ezra Stiles to Count Francesco dal Verme.

For subsidization of research I am indebted to the American Philosophical Society for two grants from the Penrose Fund and to West Virginia University for a summer grant.

I wish to thank Beverley Starr for her efficiency and patience in typing the manuscript.

ELIZABETH COMETTI

Morgantown, West Virginia
August 1968

Contents

Acknowledgments	v
Introduction	ix
The Traveler	xi
The Tour of America	xxvi
Editorial Note	xxxii
The Journal and Letters of Count Francesco dal Verme	1
1. From Falmouth to New York	3
2. The Middle States and New England	7
3. The Southern States	46
4. From Charleston to Saint John's	62
5. The West Indies	63
Appendixes	87
I Expenses on a Tour to Crown Point	89
II Letter of Ezra Stiles	91
III Letters of Luigi Castiglioni	92
Notes	95
Index	137

Illustrations

Count Francesco dal Verme *frontispiece*

between pages 14 and 15

Count Antonio and Countess Maria Camilla
   Taverna dal Verme
General George Washington
Major General Philip Schuyler
Winter cantonment of American Army
Indian family

between pages 30 and 31

Boston, 1779
Yale College

between pages 62 and 63

Ephrata Cloister
John Bartram's house

between pages 78 and 79

Old Capitol, Richmond
Plan of Halifax, N.C.
Charleston, S.C., 1780
Basse-Terre, 1780

Maps

Route of Francesco dal Verme	*page*
July–October 1783	9
October–December 1783	48
January–May 1784	65

Introduction

Introduction

The Traveler   The handsome, well-dressed young passenger who had disembarked from the English packet *Roebuck* on its arrival in New York, June 30, 1783, was Count Francesco dal Verme of Milan, Italy, as the *Royal Gazette* informed the public two days later.[1] The voyage from Falmouth, England, had been quite satisfactory, although it had taken the *Roebuck* forty-seven days to cross the Atlantic. The ship was remarkably clean and well-appointed; its officers were experienced and genial; and it had a good table, a well-stocked cellar, and a fair library. Accompanying the Count was his efficient manservant who, like his master, spoke several languages and was blessed with a sturdy constitution.

It was not uncommon at this time for young men of high station to make a "grand tour" prior to settling down to marriage and family. Usually, though, the tour covered the Old World capitals and historic sites, not America, whose main attractions were its green vastness and its aborigines. During the Revolution, America had seen a great influx of Europeans — British and French troops, German mercenaries, soldiers of fortune, and agents of one kind or another. When the war ended, the flow of foreigners continued. Most of them came to settle in the new country, but others came to collect debts, retrieve lands, reunite with relatives and friends, spread the gospel, find political asylum, and even to escape the gallows.[2] None of these motives brought Count dal Verme to America. He simply wanted to see the country and meet its leading people, particularly General George Washington.

Having been assured in London that the English would have evacuated New York by the time of his arrival there, Count dal Verme did not bring letters of introduction to British officials in that city. But he did have letters from William Franklin and from the American peace commissioners, Henry Laurens, Benjamin Franklin, and John Adams, which he had obtained through the courtesy of family connections in banking and diplomatic circles.[3] Signor Gandolfi of London and Messieurs Caccia and Grand of Paris — the first was Dal Verme's banker and postal agent — had been very helpful.[4] So had the Count's uncle by marriage, Giacomo d'Aquino, Prince Caramanico, who was the Neapolitan ambassador at the Court of St. James; Count Lodovico Belgioioso, the Austrian ambassador at London, who was a compatriot of the Milanese traveler; and Belgioioso's successor, Count Friedrich Kageneck.[5]

The indispensable letters of introduction were all of a type: whether or not the writer was personally acquainted with him, the bearer was invariably represented as a man worthy of whatever attentions the recipient might wish to confer. Certainly no favor was more welcome to the traveler than the addition of another name to the valuable round robin that ensured hospitality in a strange country. Dr. Franklin's letter in behalf of Count dal Verme was typical of this genre:

The Count Dal Verme, an Italian nobleman of great distinction, does me the honor to be the bearer of this. I have not the satisfaction to be personally acquainted with this gentleman, but I am much solicited by some of my particular friends, to whom his merits and character are known, to afford him this introduction to you. He is, I understand, a great traveller, and his view in going to America is merely to see the country and its great men. I pray you will show him every civility, and afford him that counsel, which, as a stranger, he may stand in need of.[6]

Genealogy had little interest for eighteenth-century Americans. Land or an equivalent asset, not lineage, counted for self-advancement, were it in politics, business, or marriage. Still, the New World patriciate liked to display the family crest, if they could possible lay claim to one, on their carriages, their servants' livery, their plate, their walking sticks, their tombs.[7] Although the Americans were to interdict the bestowal of titles of nobility—they doubtless saw the incongruity of elected bodies assuming this royal prerogative—they were nonetheless impressed by such marks of distinction.

Had one of these Americans inquired of Count dal Verme the origin of the family name and arms, he would have replied that he was not certain which had come first. Legend had it that the name was derived from a deed of valor performed by some unknown ancestor in the valley of the Adige—the slaughter of a dreadful serpent, a *verme* of such unusual size and features that it resembled a dragon, one of those lively, ubiquitous dragons that became extinct with the passing of the Middle Ages. In any case, the crest of the Dal Verme coat of arms is an embowed arms, sinister, holding a double-chained dragon, erased.[8]

Verona was the *patria* of this distinguished family. There, in 1226, Nicola dal Verme was striving along with other Guelfic leaders to revive and strengthen the Lombard League against the aggressive designs of Frederick II. Nicola's son, Bonaventura, was elected podesta of Cerea in 1257. His son, another Nicola, twice became podesta of Bergamo; and the grandson, Pietro, became successively podesta of Lucca, Bassano, and Treviso and, finally, governor of Verona.[9]

All of these men were soldiers as well as magistrates, bold adventurers in the service of first one, then another of the ambitious lords of northern Italy whose names—Scaligeri, Visconti, Gonzaga, Sforza—are now remembered more as builders and as patrons of art than as rulers. But, for them the role of maecenas was of minor importance; since they depended on force to retain and enhance their powers they bestowed high honors and rich feudatories on the successful condottieri. Luchino dal Verme served the Scaligeri, the Visconti, and the Republic of Venice, whose empire stretched to the Levant. Fighting against the Guelfs from 1356 to 1364, Luchino took Pavia in 1359 and began there the construction of the turreted Castello Visconteo that still dominates the city. His greatest exploit was the defeat of the Venetian secessionists on the island of Candia (Crete) in 1364, for which he was handsomely rewarded by the Adriatic Republic. It was Petrarch who had recommended Luchino to Doge Lorenzo Celsi for the Cretan expedition. The great humanist had come to know and admire Luchino in Milan, and to him the poet dedicated his treatise *De officio et virtutibus imperatoris*. When Petrarch heard of Luchino's death (1372) in Syria, where Luchino had gone to fight the Turks, he sent a tender message to the bereaved son, Jacopo: "I read your letter, my son, and from it I experienced a strange bittersweet feeling, as I sighed over the memory of so great a friend, whom I wish and hope and urge that you might be like. If this comes to pass, all of his friends, and I above all, will be immensely happy." [10]

The son proved to be even more successful than the father. Under the standard of Gian Galeazzo Visconti, Jacopo took town after town and crossed swords with the greatest condottieri. Jacopo's defeat of Count Armagnac at Alessandria was commemorated in verse by Ariosto and in stone by the proud victor with the erection of the temple of San Giacomo della Vittoria at Alessandria. Upon losing favor at the Milanese court, Jacopo transferred his services to the Venetian Republic with the intention of engaging the Turks in the Levant, as his father had done, but he died in 1409 without realizing his plans. To his family he left an enriched patrimony scattered over northern Italy and membership in the patriciates of Milan, Pavia, and Venice.

As captain of his father's veterans, Luigi served the Venetians, the Bolognese, and the Duke of Milan, who invested him with the feudatories of Bobbio, Voghera, and Castel San Giovanni. In 1433 the Emperor Sigismund further extended the Dal Verme holdings and conferred on the family both the title of count and the right to add the red and silver colors of Hungary to the azure and silver bars on the family arms.

Pietro dal Verme, Luigi's son, had the misfortune to be caught in the vicious power struggle within the House of Sforza. The ascendancy of Ludovico, "Il Moro," to the dukedom of Milan brought heavy confiscations that included the Dal Verme palace in Milan. Pietro's death in 1485 from poison administered, so tradition has it, by his second wife, Chiara Sforza, left Taddeo, his brother, as the defender of the family's still considerable possessions.

The alliance between the Milanese duke and the French king, Charles VIII, lowered the drawbridge to foreign intervention and further increased the insecurity of life and property in northern Italy. Marcantonio dal Verme, Taddeo's son, was twice condemned to death, first by Il Moro, then by the French conquerors of Milan; three times he was despoiled of his properties, once by Il Moro and twice by the French. Yet when the indomitable Marcantonio died in 1538 he was able to pass on to his heirs by his wife, Ippolita, daughter of Count Lodovico Visconti-Borromeo, some valuable feudatories that had been properly confirmed by the respective suzerains, Emperor Charles V, Pope Clement VII, and the Duke of Milan.

Francesco, who died in 1578, was the last of the Dal Verme condottieri. His son, Ercole (1564–1632), disillusioned by the perfidy in high places, set the pattern which his descendants were to follow by dedicating himself to the cultivation of his lands, to the care of his many children, and to being a good son of the Church.

"It is no longer the old and is not yet the new," Count Antonio dal Verme (1709–90) might have said of Milanese society in his own century, the enlightened, the optimistic eighteenth. In the Accademia dei Trasformati, of which Count Antonio and his brother, Abbot Pietro, were members, the old and the new intellectual currents blended to produce a rare variety of interests ranging from the venerated classics to the most audacious scientific and political theories.[11]

The Italian nationalism that would explode in the next century was still dormant in this twilight period of the old regime. Lombardy, one of the choicest of the Hapsburg dominions, was governed by Count Karl Joseph Firmian, who faithfully implemented the reform program instituted by Emperor Joseph II and his astute chancellor, Prince Kaunitz. Firmian found the social climate of the Lombard capital highly congenial; its music—La Scala was inaugurated in 1778, its art, its libraries, its sophisticated society appealed to the cultivated Austrian governor. During his long period of service in Lombardy he collected thousands of books and prints that eventually enriched the cultural endowment of Milan. His relations with the Milanese nobility were good and were kept so by the judicious conferral of favors and honors.[12] No doubt he was responsible for the nomination of his friend Count Antonio dal Verme as Chamberlain of the House of Austria in 1771.

Count Antonio dal Verme was a learned, very serious, and somewhat provincial man; for him Milan was the center of the universe. In 1750 he married Maria Camilla Taverna, daughter of Count Costanzo Taverna, by whom he had ten children. Three of them died in childhood; one, a daughter, was an invalid; one became a nun. Margherita, the firstborn, married Marquis Carlo Francesco Visconti, and her younger sister, Anna, married Count Cesare Giulini. Francesco, the oldest of the three sons to reach manhood, was born on June 28, 1758, and died April 17, 1832.[13]

The distinguished genealogist of famous Italian families, Pompeo Litta, has little to say about Francesco dal Verme other than that he was noted for his travels in America, where he came to know Washington, and that he received an honorary degree in law from the "Accademia d'Yall in Nuovo Porto provincia di Connecticut," in 1783. In 1791 Francesco married Maria, the daughter of Count Lorenzo Taverna, who bore him twelve children, seven sons and five daughters. Four of the sons traveled widely, two of them visiting the United States and other parts of America.[14]

Count Francesco was in the United States when anti-British feeling was still high and conversation invariably turned on the eight long years of war. As one of Washington's traveling companions on the lonely New York frontier and as a guest in the homes of many Revolutionary leaders, the Count must have heard endless political discussion, much of it flavored with the confident liberalism of the new republic. Yet there is no evidence that his American experience altered his basically conservative political convictions or thrust him into the vanguard of the Risorgimento.

The testing time for Count Francesco came with the French Revolution when Napoleon, in collaboration with Italian Jacobins, swept away the existing Italian states and replaced them with ephemeral republics which in their turn were destroyed to create the short-lived Kingdom of Italy. In Lombardy the middle class observed the fall of the old order with general satisfaction, but the nobility, concerned as it was with the preservation of its property and privileges, was divided. A minority faction supported French intervention in the hope that it might lead to national fulfillment; the second group, politically experienced and dedicated to the preservation of ethnic purity, had no use for the foreigner or his revolutionary principles. Neither group gained ascendancy during the period of French domination, for Napoleon favored first one, then the other, and treated both as vassals.[15]

In the two decades of upheaval, Count Francesco dal Verme managed to remain aloof from political involvement, a feat which must have required consummate adroitness. Yet his cousin Giuseppe Taverna, the "Beppo" mentioned with so much affection in the Count's letters from America, was a member of the Justice Department of the Cisalpine Republic and in 1805 he was made the president of the Corps Legislatif of the Kingdom of Italy. Perhaps Dal Verme simply "excused" himself from participation in the satellite governments of Italy, as did some members of the Lombard patriciate.[16]

Dal Verme's abstention from politics, though, was balanced by social activism.[17] Following his example, his descendants turned their attention to the professions, agronomy, education, and, of course, the arts. One of them transformed an ordinary playhouse into an elegant theatre, the Teatro Dal Verme, that almost vied with La Scala in the quality of its lyric performances. Here Giacomo Puccini gained his earliest plaudits; and here on May 21, 1892, Arturo Toscanini directed the first performance of *I Pagliacci*.[18] But let us return to Count Francesco.

"From the oppertunities I have had to form an opinion of him," George Washington wrote of Count dal Verme in 1783, "[he] is very deserving of attention."[19] Obviously the General must have liked the affable Count to have had him as his guest on four different occasions. The Italian encountered the same cordiality in

British-occupied New York, in New England, in Philadelphia, in the South, and in the English and French West Indies. Yale College awarded him an honorary degree after he had known President Stiles only a few hours. Surely such exuberant hospitality was not entirely due to credentials, excellent though they were.

As befitting a man of good breeding Count dal Verme displayed a fine sense of delicacy in the observance of the amenities. George Washington, his host during two weeks of strenuous touring in New York State, spent a considerable sum for tavern accommodations, food, horse hire, and ferryage, even though the General's party was entertained at several stopping points en route and fished for its supper on Lake Champlain. Since it would have been embarrassing to insist on paying his share of expenses, on his return to New York the Count left fifty guineas with a friend of Washington's; informed of the gift, the General asked that it be applied to the purchase of a pipe of wine for consignment to Mount Vernon.[20] It is, of course, impossible to know in what manner, if at all, the Italian thanked the scores of Americans who entertained him, but he did prepare a long list of names preceded by the notation, "I have to thank them for the courtesies shown me"; and before he left Charleston, South Carolina, for the West Indies, he paid a number of farewell visits.

The acceptance of hospitality imposed an obligation to return it upon request, and with the increasing interest in travel, in the grand tour that every young man yearned to make, one never knew when he would be asked to requite some past kindness. Although Milan was not one of the main stations for travelers, its flourishing culture, its healthy industry, and, above all, its rich agriculture attracted a few Americans, among them Thomas Jefferson in 1787 and Thomas Lee Shippen and John Rutledge, Jr., the following year. Their hosts in Lombardy were Count dal Verme and Count Luigi Castiglioni, both of whom had received many courtesies in America. Castiglioni had just returned from there with copious notes for his book, *Viaggio Negli Stati Uniti dell'America Settentrionale*, a fine herbarium, and a variety of seeds and roots which he planted on his estate not far from Milan.[21]

Both Milanese discharged their social obligations with exquisite consideration for their guests' interests and tastes. The serious-minded American Minister to France, squire of Monticello, amateur architect, and irrepressible fancier of mechanical devices, went with Dal Verme outside Milan to see how cheese was made, how rice was processed, and how icehouses were constructed. He received information on wages, prices, and tenancy. He admired the palazzi of the Lombard capital, especially Casa Roma, Casa Candiani, and Casa Belgioioso, whose salon he regarded as "superior" to anything he had seen. He listened attentively to Dal Verme's description of a pendulum odometer for the wheel of a carriage and to accounts of the variable local weather which had been known to produce hailstones large enough to kill cats.[22]

Thirty-five years later, Jefferson still recalled with pleasure his visit to the Lombard countryside. Writing to Maria Cosway, once the toast of Jefferson's circle in Paris, now the preceptress of a select school for girls at Lodi, the aged statesman reminisced: "I was in that place in 1786 [1787] with a good friend, the Count del Verme of Milan, and past a whole day, from sunrise to sunset, in a dairy there to see the process of making Parmesan cheese." Mrs. Cosway was pleased that Jefferson approved of her decision to establish her college at Lodi, a quiet, pretty place removed from the bustle of this world. "I know well all the family Del Vermi," she added, "& have their children in my establishment, one is just going to be married to one of the first Noblemen here."[23]

On his return from southern France and northern Italy to Paris in the summer of 1787, Jefferson graciously thanked Count dal Verme for his favors and gave him the latest news from America: a constitutional convention with Washington as its president was meeting in Philadelphia, and the "commotions" in Massachusetts that had recently shaken the young republic were over. Jefferson also sent three books to his Milanese host—*Notes on the State of Virginia*, Ramsay's *History of the Revolution of South-Carolina*, and Soulès' *Histoire des troubles de l'Amérique anglaise*—the first work, the Virginian explained, "because it was my own, and [the] two others because worth reading."[24]

The American minister was so pleased with the "attentions & services" he had received in Lombardy that he directed other Americans to Count dal Verme. "The readiness with which you were so kind as to shew me what was most worth seeing in Milan & it's neighborhood when I had the honour of seeing you there," Jefferson wrote him the year following his visit, "encourages me to address to you two of my young countrymen who will pass thro' Milan in a tour they are taking."[25] The two travelers, still in their early twenties, were Thomas Lee Shippen, son of Dr. William Shippen of Philadelphia and nephew of Richard Henry Lee of

Virginia, and John Rutledge, Jr., son of Governor John Rutledge of South Carolina and nephew of Edward Rutledge, a signer of the Declaration of Independence. To facilitate their travels, Jefferson obligingly prepared a little guidebook for the young men in which he urged them to give special attention to the agriculture, manufacturing, landscaping, architecture, and politics of the countries they visited. He suggested that while in Milan they make an excursion to Rozzano to inspect its dairy industry and method of storing snow; from there they should proceed to Pavia to feast their eyes on the abbey of Certosa, the "richest thing" Jefferson had ever seen.

What really captivated the two Americans, though, and made them loath to leave the Lombard capital was not its economy or its architecture, but its gay and brilliant society. Dal Verme and Castiglioni took them in hand and introduced them to every luminary, from the renowned Marquis Cesare Beccaria to the Countess Amelia Litta, whose Friday evening receptions attracted all of "the first women of Milan." Both Shippen and Rutledge were enchanted with this beautiful and accomplished woman, and both were intrigued by her unconventional, "almost incredible" conversation.[26]

The hub of the Milanese *haut monde* was, very appropriately, the opera house, La Scala, where, in addition to good music, all kinds of conversation might be heard. The social day began at four in the afternoon with a dinner *en famille*. At five the members of this charmed circle got into their handsomest carriages and drove to the *corso* where they moved about "looking and bowing" at each other. At six they went to the Cathedral Square to refresh themselves with ices until time for the theatre. At La Scala everyone had his own elegantly appointed box, large enough to accommodate as many as twenty or thirty persons, according to Shippen. Opposite these little salons were small rooms where servants prepared chocolate, lemonade, syrups, and other drinks for their masters and guests. The ladies generally sat in the front seats of the boxes, so that the men who sat next to them had the double advantage of being able to see the stage and to converse with a charming lady. After a little time in this enviable situation, the polite gentleman relinquished his place to some newcomer to the box and betook himself to another little salon. Thus, "by managing well," young Shippen explained to his father, "particularly if you are a stranger, you may sit next a fair woman, see and hear the opera, and also change the scene continually for 4 hours every Evening."[27]

This was the singularly pleasant milieu of which Count Francesco dal Verme took leave in 1782 for a grand tour of France, the British Isles, and far-off America.

Contin Francesco, as he was often called, departed from Milan on March 5, 1782, for Genoa, where he planned to take ship for Marseilles. His father had warned him not to embark at Leghorn because it was under constant danger from corsairs, but the young man could not resist a quick visit to that seaport and nearby Pisa and Lucca before leaving Italy. During these first days from home, he must have often reflected on his father's *promemoria* replete with paternal concern and affection.[28] Contin Francesco was to write home at least once a week and keep a diary. He should sail only on large vessels because they were safe from the scourge of pirates. He should pause at Nice and Antibes, two spots well worth visiting. In case of illness he should put himself under the care of accredited doctors and surgeons, whose names he could obtain from local bankers. On his arrival at a place he should immediately get in touch with the resident minister or the Austrian consul. To avoid incurring any kind of suspicion when visiting military sites such as fortresses and arsenals, he should always be accompanied by some dignitary. When stopping at inns he should have his servant sleep in the same room with him and see that the door was locked; valises as well as doors should always be locked. He should be careful of the kind of porters he hired to use as guides.

For practical reasons, above all in order to devote as much time as possible to sightseeing, Contin Francesco originally planned to travel incognito and thus avoid the *gran mondo*. But while still in Genoa he found that it would be impossible to remain entirely aloof from society, so he requested his father to send him one dark and one lightweight suit; the first embroidered in gold; the second, in silver.

Arrived at Marseilles in late April, the young count reiterated to his father his travel procedure before asking permission to proceed from Lyon, his original destination, or so his father thought, to Paris; to be in France and miss Paris would be like going to Rome and not see the Pope, the son remarked. He assured his father that the proposed extension of his tour would not require additional funds, since he had managed to keep his expenses below the amount anticipated; to be precise, in fifty days of travel, he had already "saved" 22 sequins. He also asked his father to apply to Count Firmian for a letter of introduction to the Imperial Minister at

Paris, Count Florimond-Claude Mercy-Argenteau. Firmian had offered such a letter at the time Contin Francesco had gone to pay his farewell respects; consequently there would be no trouble in obtaining one.

By mid-May Contin Francesco was at Avignon. He arrived in early June at Lyon, where by happy coincidence he received mail from his father enclosing various letters of presentation for Paris, including the desired one from Firmian. In July he was at Paris, a crowded city with muddy streets and many cabarets and theatres, Contin Francesco told his father, a city offering every kind of cultural opportunity—libraries, academies, universities, museums, botanical gardens, scientific laboratories, and art schools. After several weeks in Paris, during which time he saw a number of friends and had dinner with Count Mercy, Francesco solicited his father's permission to extend his journey to London, really only a jaunt from the French capital and a much more interesting place than the latter, so everyone said. Again he assured Count Antonio that such a visit would not require additional funds. His unpretentious mode of living in Paris—a room with an alcove for the servant instead of a large apartment, an occasional fiacre instead of a private carriage, an ordinary servant instead of one in livery, dinner at a common instead of a private table—and his circumspection had enabled him to make some substantial savings. Lest Count Antonio think that modest accommodations were unbefitting a Milanese nobleman, Francesco assured him that his table companions were either Knights of St. Louis or foreigners of rank. To his continuing requests the young man usually appended gossip about Milanese friends and various news calculated to interest his father.

On August 25, Contin Francesco set out for London, although he had not yet received his father's permission to extend his travels. With the excuse, however, that in anticipation of an affirmative answer he had reserved a seat on the diligence, he proceeded to Ostend, crossed the Channel to Margate, and arrived in London on the last day of the month. His lodgings in the English capital consisted of two rooms, one for himself and one for his servant. Shortly after his arrival he witnessed the hanging of six men, three of whom had preferred death to a life of hard labor in America. On a visit to Portsmouth he saw the armada under Admiral Lord Richard Howe set sail for Gibraltar and heard about the futile efforts to bring up the *Royal George,* an old and rotten ship which had tilted and sunk at Spithead with heavy loss of lives, including those of many women and children.[29] September fogs were beginning to envelop London, but the weather in general was still good enough to warrant a visit to the countryside.

The casual excursion turned out to be a trip of 388 miles in a diligence that took him to Edinburgh in less than four days, with pauses for sight-seeing en route. Having provided himself with a letter for Lord Prevost, he lost no time in becoming acquainted with Scotland from Edinburgh to Glasgow.[30] Besides the hospitable Prevost, he visited the Duke of Buccleuch, the Marquess of Lothian, Lord Hopetoun, and the Duke of Hamilton, whose picture gallery contained a Rubens masterpiece, *Daniel in the Lions' Den*.[31] He talked with businessmen, prelates, academicians, two Bolognese visitors, and some French prisoners of war. He descended into a coal mine, dark as the catacombs, where many men and women were working, and inspected a munitions factory. He visited the imposing castle of Edinburgh, the Royal Academy, the botanical gardens, and the hospitals. He saw Stirling Castle, the remains of the Roman wall of Antoninus, and the textile works at Paisley. He also witnessed some heroic drinking bouts which necessitated special facilities for relief. In short, Contin Francesco's sojourn in Scotland, which he described for his sister in a journal written in French, was packed with new experiences.

Upon his return from Scotland in October, Contin Francesco immediately set off for Ireland.[32] Here a letter from the Marquise Castiglione to Lord Jocelyn initiated a round robin that provided entree to the imposing estates of Irish peers.[33] He saw everything worth seeing in Dublin, including its college, government buildings, gardens, and theatres. He visited the sublimely beautiful lakes of Killarney and the castle at Kilkenny. At Limerick he attended a dinner given by the garrison in honor of General John Burgoyne.[34] At Cork he noted its extensive commerce in meat and dairy products. Such was the hospitality of the Irish that he "never dined, never supped, never breakfasted in hotels, except when traveling." The climate of Ireland, though, was very damp, and the wretched condition of the tenantry, victims of absentee landlords, was positively depressing. These ragged peasants lived with their animals in miserable windowless clod houses no higher than a man. Beggars were everywhere, particularly in front of Catholic churches. On the ship back to England he was unable to find sleeping accommodations and was obliged to crouch like a dog for thirty hours.

"I only lack the language and libertinism to be English; I am here to learn the first and with reason I hope not to fall into the second," Contin Francesco wrote from London to his sister in early December. With his customary intensity, he availed himself of every opportunity to master the language, going so far as to hire a new laundress because the old one spoke English badly. He finally decided to pass the remainder of the winter in a college at Hampstead where he could receive professional instruction and talk with other lodgers, some of whom were foreigners like himself. Count Antonio thought that his son was going too far with his linguistic aspirations. Why should a Milanese nobleman bother to study English, since French was the universal language and all the best English writings were available in translation? It looked as if, on one pretext or another, Contin Francesco intended to prolong his travels from year to year; next he would be asking leave to visit America—this in spite of the sad fact that his brother Carlo had recently died.

Count Antonio's suspicions were entirely justified. On February 7, 1783, his son launched his long-contemplated assault to obtain permission to go to America. His arguments, interspersed with professions of filial love and gratitude for past forbearance, were carefully selected. Now that the Revolutionary War was over, one could cross the Atlantic in safety without convoy. To be sure, a Milanese living far from the sea might be apprehensive about such a voyage, but not an Englishman, accustomed to seeing daily transatlantic departures and arrivals. A brief tour of America would entail no more time and expense than the visit to Flanders and the Netherlands he had thought of making; he would certainly be home by the end of 1783. His honest desire to see the New World and General Washington before settling down to marriage and family responsibilities was no just cause for reproach; on the other hand, the frustration of his honest passion for traveling might some day bring remorse to Count Antonio. So back and forth, between London and Milan, went the arguments and rebuttals until the father capitulated on condition that the son return to Italy by the end of the spring of 1784.

Contin Francesco could not have won this victory without allies, especially without the secret and very loyal collaboration of his sister Margherita Visconti. "Ghitta" was his confidante, his advocate, his mentor; it was she who arranged for substantial loans of money to be forwarded to her brother in Paris and London and who reviewed the arguments to be presented to "Il Principale." For the truth was that Count Francesco kept two sets of epistolary books, one for his father and one for his sister, and it was the latter that told the story straight, without dissimulation. While still in Marseilles he had written her that he intended to sail for the Antilles—a plan that had to be abandoned because he was unable to find passage—and that he would no longer travel incognito because of his persistent loneliness. She knew that his vaunted economies were only trifling and that his dedication to self-improvement was not so exclusive as to prevent his enjoyment of the *haut monde* of the French capital, where his stay of fifty-six days had seemed no more than a week. And to her he rehearsed in detail his strategy for the gradual reduction of his father's opposition, his own formidable "Gibraltar," as he called it.

These disclosures probably caused Ghitta to ring for her smelling salts whenever one of her brother's letters arrived. He, of course, made light of her fears for his safety on the seas, telling her that she should see how many old tars were still around. As for his ability to finance the journey, he assured her that his expenses would be slight; he had recently read in an English newspaper that a family could live more comfortably in America on 100 lire than in England on 500 lire. And of course, if he should run short of funds, "alors, alors à la maison." Why all the criticism? "Dio Santo," he was not proposing anything wrong. If he were going to America in search of wealth, he would receive general approbation; or if his present wretchedness stemmed from some misfortune, he would be the object of compassion. Instead. . . . Enough of this tempest. One's parent simply did not give an absolute veto to a man of twenty-five.

The "epidemic of letters" subsided in March 1783, when the long-sought permission arrived together with a subsidy of 234 lire sterling to be made available either in cash or in letters of credit.[35] Very prudently the son chose the latter. Once his *destino* had been decided, the young man happily plunged into preparations for his new adventure. Gandolfi, the banker who was taking care of the financial details, gave him much advice, offered to procure letters of recommendation, and agreed to forward all mail to and from America. Count Francesco interviewed Americans to secure information and obtained from the Austrian and Neapolitan ambassadors letters for prominent Americans and for the foreign ministers at Philadelphia. He learned that the two best means of going to

America were by merchant vessel to Boston or by packet—one of which left England the first Wednesday of each month—to New York. Since the mail ship required only a month for the voyage, half a month less than a Boston-bound merchantman, Count Francesco decided to take passage on the speedier vessel. Assuming that he would not need an elaborate wardrobe in America, he shipped to Milan a trunk containing five of his most elegant suits, four coats, and other apparel, all of his servant's livery, some English books for "Beppo" Taverna who was studying that language, a pair of pistols, and a gift for his father. In transacting the inevitable last-minute business, the Count was ably assisted by his servant Bordone, who had acquired some knowledge of French and English since his departure from Italy. The two left London on May 6, 1783, and arrived at Falmouth on the 10th. Three days later came the dispatches from the Secretariat; the following day, May 14, the packet *Roebuck* set sail at 3 o'clock in the afternoon under a favorable wind. Before boarding the vessel, Contin Francesco wrote to his father and sister describing with muted enthusiasm the fine accommodations on the ship, of which he was the only passenger. But it carried some milch goats and plenty of chickens, ducks, and suckling pigs to provide fresh meat at table. He told his father that he had letters of recommendation from London and Paris for General Washington, members of Congress, and other personages in the United States. To his sister he sent a statement of his resources with the reassurance that his supply of money was adequate for his sojourn in America, where he did not expect to buy a single item of clothing or spend anything on entertainment.[36] And so he set sail.

In his own fashion Count Francesco kept the promises that he made to his father. He wrote long letters with some regularity from the United States and the West Indies, and he prepared a journal which covered most, but not all, of his travels. He did not arrive in Milan by the end of spring, but he did start homeward from Havana on May 9, 1784. As usual, he had various explanations for his delay, all of them valid enough. He had, in truth, become impatient to be reunited with his family and friends from whom he had received no news for almost a year.[37] His return voyage of forty-three days on a Spanish brigantine which averaged seven miles an hour was "felicissimo," despite strong winds and turbulent seas, so he informed his father less than two hours after debarking at Santander. But when he reached home and was the hero of the hour, he doubtless gave the same account of the crossing that he wrote to a friend in America: "My passage home on board of the postillione di St. Andrea has been three and forty days, and lucky enough. Nastiness, olia, rotten peases, rotten salt'd fish, rotten bread, and spoiled Catalonian wine have always been in plenty; luckily for me I had my provision of jamaica Rum otherwise their damn'd Avana Canneta should have been my drinking. The officers of the customhouse as well as those of the Inquisition at St. Andrera in Biscay have been very kind to us, the former not having searched in our pockets, the latter having depended upon our word that we were not circumcised." [38] He left Santander on June 24, and going by way of Bilbao, Bayonne, Bordeaux, and Montauban reached Toulouse on July 6. Here he had the very good fortune to meet Count Luigi Castiglioni, who was en route to England and America and who informed him that Dal Verme's family and friends in Milan were all well.[39] By July 15, the veteran traveler was at Genoa, having come there by sea from Antibes. Two days later, he reached Milan.

The Tour of America   The United States of America was seeing "sundry learned and intelligent men" during the triumphant days following the Revolution, reported the German scientist Dr. Johann David Schoepf. "Germans, Swedes, French, English, Dutch and even an Italian *conte,* were present to muse upon the wonders of the new states, and they journeyed almost always with pen or black-lead in their hands." "But now," he continued, "after the passage of several years, none of them has been pleased to give to the public the results of his observations, if I except the brief reports of Professor Martyr. . . . It may be that the others were deceived in their expectations, not finding memorable things in the hoped-for plenitude, and have done what I perhaps should have done." [40] Despite what Schoepf said, in the course of time some of these travel accounts were published,[41] but the one written by the Italian count, who was, of course, Francesco dal Verme, remained in the Dal Verme Archives and was read only by the family and an occasional scholar.

The truth is that, unlike the other tourists equipped with writing materials, Dal Verme never had the slightest intention of offering for publication his journal and letters from abroad. His was an exclusive record, written solely for his family's information and pleasure. The contents, he confided to his favorite sister, Margherita, were intentionally inoffensive and devoid of "anything arresting." [42] The journal was kept as a matter of filial duty, to reassure his relatives in far-off Milan that he was faring well, covering much ground, and meeting many distinguished Americans. So with scrupulous regularity he noted meals, lodgings, mileage, weather, and important names. One suspects that, unlike his compatriot Luigi Castiglioni, Dal Verme arrived in America with only such superficial knowledge of the place as might be gleaned from newspapers and conversations with American expatriates. Yet this lack of preparation was not without advantage: it spared him from the charge of plagiarizing, of being too "gazetteer-ish," of pretending to have seen what he had not. It reduced his journal to bare, self-oriented narrative.

While it is just as well that Dal Verme did not digress from his own personal experiences, it is regrettable that he did not enrich his account of them with vivid detail. He was with General Washington for more than two weeks, riding with him along the New York frontier, sailing with him on Lake Champlain, eating with him, camping with him, seeing him acclaimed and memorialized, yet he gives no hint of what the great man said or did during this summer excursion. Did Washington reprimand the soldiers whose carelessness deprived the party of a feast on mutton? Did he discuss politics or war? Did he complain about travel conditions? Did he sustain the lighthearted mood in which he started on the tour? Did he comment on the terms of peace? Here the lack of particulars is especially disappointing because scant as it is, Dal Verme's record of the trip is still the best source of information we have on it. Dal Verme also did not take the trouble to describe the personages he met, not even Washington, whom other reporters were always careful to portray.

The Milanese count did a little better by the women, but unlike most of the Latin travelers, particularly the French, he did not descant on the ladies' appearance—their tall, erect bodies, their fine hair, their bad teeth, their ephemeral beauty, their innocent charm. Only two of the many American belles he met received special attention, Mrs. John Langdon and the talented Betsey Hunter.

Dal Verme also had little to say about American mores and manners, and nothing at all about relations between the sexes or about social equality, on which other foreign observers were prone to dwell. Gossip he avoided—and he must have heard some piquant stories—except for passing reference to the Hitchbourn case, which kept Massachusetts tongues wagging for months.

Not until he reached the West Indies did Dal Verme display any repugance for slavery, although he had traveled through all of the continental states where that institution was rooted in the economy. The numerical preponderance of the Negro population on the sugar islands, the severity of the slave codes, the distinctive customs and dress of these people greatly impressed the Milanese visitor. As far as West Indian planter society was concerned, he dismissed it with a shrug; there was nothing to it.

Despite the discomforts he endured from time to time in the course of his journey, an undercurrent of good humor runs through all of Dal Verme's journal and letters. Even while struggling over the miserable roads and bridges of North Carolina and pausing for refreshments at the dirty hovels that passed for inns, he never indulged in the captious outbursts that came from some travelers through that area. Invariably he made the best of a bad situation, and he sometimes joked about it. Twice he was the victim of theft, in London and at Cap-Français, but in neither instance did he bemoan his losses—at least not in writing.[43] And his high spirits persisted through the return voyage on a dirty Spanish brigantine and on the overland ride back to Milan.

Carrying no chip on his shoulder and having no axe to grind, Dal Verme was never rancorous or tendentious. If he occasionally referred to the British as the "enemy," that was only because he was repeating, as he frequently did, what he had just heard. With complete impartiality he moved among the Loyalists and patriots, British and French; they were all the same to the neutral Milanese.

Diverse as were the nationalities, social backgrounds, and intellectual interests of the travelers mentioned by Schoepf, they generally visited the same places; an organized tour or a popular Baedeker could scarcely have achieved more uniform sight-seeing. This similarity of itineraries was less the result of design than of the limitation of travel facilities. Although the visitor could enter the United States by way of the Saint Lawrence and Lake Champlain or through one of several busy eastern ports, most likely Boston, New York, Philadelphia, Norfolk, or Charleston, once here he had little choice of routes and modes of travel.

The post roads of New England and the Middle States were fairly good, as were the taverns along them despite the scarcity of private rooms and the annoying inquisitiveness of landlords. In this area the traveler who was encumbered with baggage or had neither horse nor private carriage could go by public stagecoach cheaply and rapidly, if not comfortably. During the winter, when snow lay thick on the ground, the diligence could be transformed into a great sledge covered with canvas to keep the shivering passengers from freezing altogether.[44] Visitors, including Dal Verme, almost unanimously advised against overland travel from Virginia to South Carolina or to Georgia.[45] Better entrust oneself to the perils of the sea than to the hazards of the southern roads.

By necessity, then, many visitors missed seeing some of the grandest natural wonders of the new nation—Niagara Falls,[46] the forested Appalachians, the confluence of the Potomac and Shenandoah, and Natural Bridge, the last two sights extolled by Jefferson in his *Notes on the State of Virginia*.[47] Instead, they contented themselves with the more accessible Cohoes Falls in New York, Passaic or Totowa Falls in New Jersey, Potomac Falls, the Palisades of the Hudson, and the islands and broad estuaries of the eastern coast.[48]

The remote location of Indian settlements also prevented many visitors from satisfying their intense desire to see the fabulous aboriginal man of America. But there was nothing—certainly not fear of a critical audience—to deter the frustrated travelers from giving the impression that they had indeed encountered the Indian. Or they could—and did—embellish their accounts with such dramatic pieces as Logan's lament or the cruel details of Cornstalk's death.[49] There were lively stories, too. Castiglioni wrote that Pocahontas went to England with the swashbuckling John Smith whose life she had saved. When the hero of early Jamestown ceased to show her either the tenderness or gratitude she deserved, the disgusted Indian princess returned to America and married a certain "Signor Roll."[50]

Completely honest and accurate, however, were the descriptions of the indigenous animals, reptiles, and birds of America, for sooner or later these creatures crossed the traveler's path, no matter how close he kept to the main-traveled routes. He noted, in particular, the raccoon, opossum, and flying squirrel; and he discovered that the prodigious rattlesnake and its relative, the copperhead, were as numerous as they were venomous.[51] He saw birds that had no classification and tasted wild fowl that was memorable. If the traveler had a scientific bent he found the continent a vast laboratory and himself pressed to catalogue all the exuberant wild life it contained.

The undisputed mecca of the new republic was Mount Vernon, where the American prophet retired at the conclusion of peace.[52] On seeing him, remarked a traveler somewhat peevishly, "children, men, and women expressed such contentment as if the Redeemer had entered Jerusalem!" It was certainly remarkable that considering how many great Americans had contributed to the success of independence, none had "either a general approbation or the popularity" of Washington; indeed, nobody had it but him.[53] In return for this incessant adulation—hardly a day passed without a visitor—Washington was obliged to provide almost continuous hospitality, there being neither a cluster of taverns nor any large towns near Mount Vernon. But he could afford it. Seeing the opulent self-sufficiency and sweeping extent of the General's estate, the visitors could not resist speculating on its annual yield and wondering who would inherit it; probably some of it would go to Mrs. Washington's grandchildren;[54] it was too bad that the General had no children.

Philadelphia was the metropolis of the United States, the London and Amsterdam of America, the Utopia of the western world. All American roads led to Philadelphia. Most foreigners thought it a pleasant city, with its regular, well-paved, well-lighted, and well-drained streets, its plain brick houses, its commercial facilities. The chief tourist attractions were the Statehouse, prison, almshouse, and, above all, the Friends' meetinghouses. Everyone, Catholic or Protestant, wanted to attend a Quaker meeting and see for himself whether it was indeed true that the seating arrangement was according to sex, that no minister exhorted the congregation, that a meeting might pass in utter silence.[55] The paintings and museum of Charles Willson Peale received no great acclaim and the "paltry," short-lived exhibit of Pierre du Simitière only passing attention.[56] But those who took the trouble to see the garden of William Bartram on the outskirts of Philadelphia generally came away impressed with the luxury of its botanical display.[57]

Some distance from Philadelphia, but still accessible to the resolute traveler, were the well-ordered Moravian communities to the north and Ephrata, seat of a strange and moribund religious order, to the west. If proof were needed that religious and social heterodoxy flourished in America, these settlers of German origin provided it. Their industry, ingenuity, and piety never failed to elicit comment from visitors amazed that any people could live out their days in such monotonous dedication to a sectarian society.

Strangers found Boston and Charleston more interesting than New York, which remained in British hands through the end of the Revolution and retained the character of an English city for a little time afterward. Boston, on the other hand, was American to the core, teeming with patriots who liked nothing better than to recall the glorious struggle against British tyranny and point out the memorable sites. Foreigners found this chauvinism positively amusing. " 'Here are the ruins of Charlestown which they [the English] reduced to ashes.' " Barbé-Marbois wrote in imitation of a Bostonian. " 'A little farther is Bunker Hill, where we killed twelve hundred of their men. Those distant woods are in the neighborhood of Lexington, where on the 20th of April 1775 the English for the first time shed the blood of their brothers. . . . These redoubts, and these entrenchments, which surround Roxbury, were raised against our tyrants. . . . This church in the middle of the city, they made into a riding school, out of hatred for the Congregationalists to whom it belongs. It is from the top of this mountain that our Washington brought about the submission of General Howe. It is in that plain, at the foot of the hill on which we are standing, that the English had their camp, and this walk, formerly lined with trees which made a wholesome shade, has been reduced by that barbarous nation to the condition which you see.' " [58]

Charleston, South Carolina, which had also nurtured patriots and suffered the ravages of war, struck visitors as being almost cosmopolitan. The hospitable planters and merchants who dominated government and society in that state imitated their European counterparts in the luxury of their homes and table, the pursuit of diversion, and the love of country life. Although some of these aristocrats had an excellent education, enhanced by foreign travel, and a taste for the fine arts, their society was more strenuous than brilliant; a stranger did not easily fit into it.[59] The chief source of wealth was the extensive cultivation of rice and indigo, an exotic plant that required painstaking processing for commercial use. The tide which forced the waters at the mouth of rivers to rise several feet daily provided the irrigation so essential to the production of rice; Negro labor did the rest. All in all, South Carolina was well worth a visit, but not a lengthy one, and certainly not during the summer months.

Since foreign travelers generally went to the same places in the young Republic, they inevitably saw many of the same people—the Langdons in Portsmouth, the Lloyds, Bowdoins, Hancocks, and Cushings in Boston; the Champlins and Hunters in Newport (they had such lovely daughters);[60] the Schuylers in Albany; the Morrises, Dickinsons, and Vaughans in Philadelphia; the Fitzhughs, Harrisons, and Banisters in Virginia; the Alstons, Bees, Moultries, and Rutledges in South Carolina. Already the names of some of these Americans, which have fattened the volumes of the *Dictionary of American Biography,* had attained sufficient distinction to be duly noted, if not correctly spelled, by the strangers. In recording the kindness of their hosts, the visitors depicted a genial, lighthearted side of eighteenth-century America, an America that liked good food, good company, good hunting, and frequent dancing.

It is this America displaying its best company manners that we see in the thin, hurriedly written journal and the letters of Count Francesco dal Verme. Perhaps if he had been older, if he had not been required to keep a record of his travels, if he had been less well received in America, if he had not covered so much ground, if he had passionately pursued some special interest, he might have written a more informative journal, but certainly not a better calendar of social events. And in name-dropping he had no equal.

Editorial Note The Dal Verme archives in Milan contain three drafts of the journal of Count Francesco. The first one, which consists of a list of places he visited, mileage covered, and an occasional terse notation—"Ticonderoga *Rattel* Snake 9 feet," "Ephrata . . . hermits," "Mr. Diggs and his Jesuit brother—Mass, Nov. 1, 1783"—was probably kept from day to day and ends abruptly on Dal Verme's arrival in Charleston, South Carolina. The second draft, the one chosen for this translation, is essentially the original framework, with details and the account of the Caribbean tour added; it cuts off at Kingston, Jamaica. The third draft is a faithful, very legible copy of the second, prepared by two amanuenses of Count Antonio, who lacked either the good sight or the patience necessary for reading his son's scribbled diary. The secretaries also made copies of some of the letters sent by the son to his father, as well as of those sent to his mother. By endorsing the letters from America with the date of their receipt, Count Antonio has provided evidence of the efficiency and speed of the eastbound transatlantic and European mail service, which could deliver a letter

Introduction xxxiii

from New York to Milan in a month and a half (July 12–August 26)!

Every effort has been made to keep the translation of the Journal and letters as literal as possible without total sacrifice of readability. Thus the sentence structure has been altered to reduce the overload of dependent clauses; a number of semicolons have been eliminated in favor of periods; and modern rules of capitalization have been used. First names, consistently omitted by Dal Verme, have been inserted in brackets, and proper names have been correctly spelled; where additions and alterations represent an educated guess, a question mark has been added in brackets. Modern equivalents of obsolete place names have also been bracketed. The few words and phrases reproduced as in the original have been italicized. Finally, no biographical information has been provided for names that are easily identifiable.

*The Journal and Letters of
Count Francesco dal Verme
1783-1784*

1. From Falmouth to New York

Falmouth, May 14, 1783

Dearest Sister:

Here I am with my last letter from Falmouth, I hope. I believe I wrote you on the 10th of this month of my arrival here. Yesterday the dispatches came from the Secretariat, and today, the wind being favorable, we shall depart at three after dinner. I am the only passenger, but the Captain, first and second mates, and the surgeon, who compose the captain's table, are the very best of company, and there is a fair library on board. Our table will always be served with fresh meat, since there is an abundant supply of chickens, ducks, and suckling pigs; we also have goats for milk. Bread is baked daily for breakfast; and there is no lack of wines or liquors. The servant has the rest of the table.

From the enclosed paper you will see how much money I have had from the date of my departure to today. You must bear in mind that B represents the outlay for fourteen months, during which time I acquired ten suits, among them a formal suit and one embroidered in silk, and many other supplies; that C takes me to America without spending a cent; and that D has to do me for only a year in places where I will not have to make a single purchase for clothing or linen, where there is no gambling, where there are no shows at English prices. This thought, I hope, will please you, since it will enable you to rest assured that I have enough to take care of my needs without having had to turn to anyone except those whom you know. You may extend my greetings to one of these persons, and ask him to relay them to the other.

In my next letter I shall have material to write, something which this one lacks, as well as the time.

Affectionate greetings for all, particularly Albert, Beppo, and Viellorito. I embrace you and remain,

Your most affectionate brother,

Francesco dal Verme

[Enclosure]

List of money had after my departure from Milan, March 5, 1782.

From Father	sequins	500	Lire Sterling		234
My own		60			25
G.		1000			503
L. [?]		300			141
From Father		200			94
From Father		500			234
	sequins	2560		A	1231

	1782	Total	A	1231
From March 5 to May 14, 1783			560	B
Paid for my passage			63	C
Letters of Credit with me			600	⎫ D
In purse			8	⎭
		A	1231 A	1231

Journal from Falmouth to New York on the Packet *Roebuck*, Capt. Richiard

1783		Month	Day	Latitude G. M.	Longitude G. M.	Miles
Always staying with *Lord Hide*		May	15	50 11	5 47	58
A	Captain *Gefris* packet bound for Antigua, and adjacent islands		16	49 00	6 00	65
			17	49 02	46 58	65
			18	47 02	9 50	155
B	Hoisted flag on separating from *Lord Hide*		19	44 57	12 50	174
C	Saw a ship three leagues away		20	42 36	15 40	190
			21	40 58	17 25	127
D	Spoke to the brigantine *Monwith* of Boston loaded with rice taken from the English bound for Lisbon		22	39 48	18 22	70
			23	38 09	20 35	144
E	Saw the Island of Santa Maria 18 leagues away		24	36 27	23 15	151
F	Saw the Island of Santa Maria 6 leagues away		25	35 38	25 10	145
			26	35 07	26 40	80
			27	34 47	27 46	58
			28	34 17	29 28	91
			29	34 00	31 14	117
			30	33 31	31 27	79
			31	32 02	31 27	89
		June	1	31 05	31 06	86
			2	29 42	31 03	85
			3	28 12	31 03	88
			4	26 39	30 57	93
			5	26 01	31 03	41
			6	25 57	32 33	81
			7	25 57	33 57	77
			8	25 36	35 55	109

(*cont. on next page*)

Journal from Falmouth to New York (cont.)

		Day	Latitude G. M.	Longitude G. M.	Miles
		9	25 30	37 55	108 [?]
		10	25 40	40 24	81
		11	25 40	42 50	130
		12	25 57	45 50	163
		13	26 00	49 14	184
		14	26 03	52 09	157
		15	25 59	54 55 [?]	150
		16	26 20	57 03	116
		17	26 35	58 33	73
G		18	27 50	59 27	95
		19	27 43	60 02	32
		20	28 10	61 07	64
		21	28 30	62 26	79
		22	29 14	64 28	110
		23	30 03	66 32	120
		24	31 08	67 36	84
		25	31 37	68 17	46
H		26	32 59	68 49	94
		27	34 57	68 38	89
I		28	36 44	69 24	76
L		29	38 10	70 10	110
M		30	40 00	71 30	124

G   Sighted a ship two leagues away

```
            71.30
           −5.47
Deg.       65.43
```

```
         3921 are
                    Deg.  65.43

Covered miles       4805
In addition because of wind  884
```

H   At midnight spoke to a brigantine of North Carolina bound for South Carolina
I   Saw a brigantine
L   Spoke to the ship, *Prince of Wales*, from London to Baltimore
M   Took soundings and found bottom at 174 feet
    At four in the morning sighted land six miles away. Fifteen hours later arrived in New York.

[Log enclosed in letter of July 12, 1783, New York; see below, pp. 38–41]

2. The Middle States and New England

July 1. I took a walk around the port which surrounds the city of New York on three sides. Nearly all of the docks—they are privately owned and rented to ship's captains by the day—are accessible even to the largest vessels.[1] Paid some visits. Dined at the home of Mr. *Steward* [Stewart?] [2] and later went to see the fort on the west side of the city, where there is a large store of artillery.[3] Spent the evening and took supper with Mr. Steward. The tavern has a large game room.[4] Fair, but very warm.

July 2. Walked along the shore as far as the road leading to Kingsbridge.[5] The countryside abounds with many kinds of fruit trees, fine vegetables, and much corn. The city is large and may have a population of fifty thousand.[6] There are many brick houses, although the finest ones have been destroyed by fire.[7] Only a few coaches circulate, but many horses and chairs.[8] The English style prevails in everything, including the mode of living. Met the commandant of the city, Mr. [Samuel] Birch.[9] I found this notice in the *Gazette: In the Roebuck Packet came passenger the Count dal Verme, a young nobleman from the Duchy of Milan in Italy, who, after having made the tour of Great Britain, proposes to visit the principal parts of this continent.*[10]

On June 21, 1783, three hundred Pennsylvania soldiers, armed and without any officers except four sergeants, went to the meeting hall of Congress in Philadelphia to ask for their pay. (Congress had discharged the troops, paying them only in notes which have no purchasing power.) When, after forty hours, the men failed to attain their objective, they departed without committing any other offense. A few days later seven privates and two of the sergeants —the other two having fled—were arrested. The Congress then moved to Princeton, forty-four miles from Philadelphia.[11]

In the evening went to the theatre to see a comedy and a farce; the troupe was fairly good, the orchestra, composed of military bands, excellent. The interior [of the theatre] is large like the one at Novara and the appointments are adequate. There were many men, but few women. A dollar (the Spanish piece is called a dollar) for the best seats, half a dollar for the others.[12] Sky overcast.

July 3. Took lodgings with a person who does not eat pork in public for religious reasons. Dined at the home of Mr. Steward; after dinner went to the military review. Rain.

July 4. Had breakfast on board the packet *Roebuck,* then left with the Captain and others for a sail around York Island, which is fourteen miles long and only two miles wide. We coasted along the eastern part of this island, west of Long Island north of which nearly all ships put out to sea. This side of York Island has many fine homes at present occupied by officers. At the northeastern end of York Island the water was so low that we were obliged to cover five miles instead of one in order to stay in the channel. At the end of it there is a bank, and as the tide was low we stepped ashore and pulled up the boat with the aid of ropes. Thus it was that I first set foot on the North American continent. We went to the house of a peasant who appeared to have once been well-to-do. Returned to the boat and passed Kingsbridge which connects York Island with the mainland. A picket from each one of the armies guarded his respective part of the bridge. I was told that the sentinels have never spoken to each other, although they both patrol the breadth of the bridge at the midway point, for fear of permitting even the slightest violation of the area under their jurisdiction.[13] When we reached the western part of the island we got out of the boat to look at some forts, important in the military operations of 1776, which are still garrisoned.[14] Crossed the Hudson River and went ashore to eat. For many miles this part of the coast consists of an almost straight line of bold limestone cliffs. After lunch returned to the island. Two miles from the city stopped at a popular public house for tea. Along the waterside saw 22 battleships, about 110 transports, and a large number of merchantmen. Fair.

July 5. In the morning went to the artillery park near a pond on the north end of the city where everyone goes ice-skating in winter.[15] Dinner, tea, and supper aboard an English vessel. Rain.

July 6. Dined at the tavern, then left by boat for Elizabeth. I disembarked two miles from the town and walked the remainder of

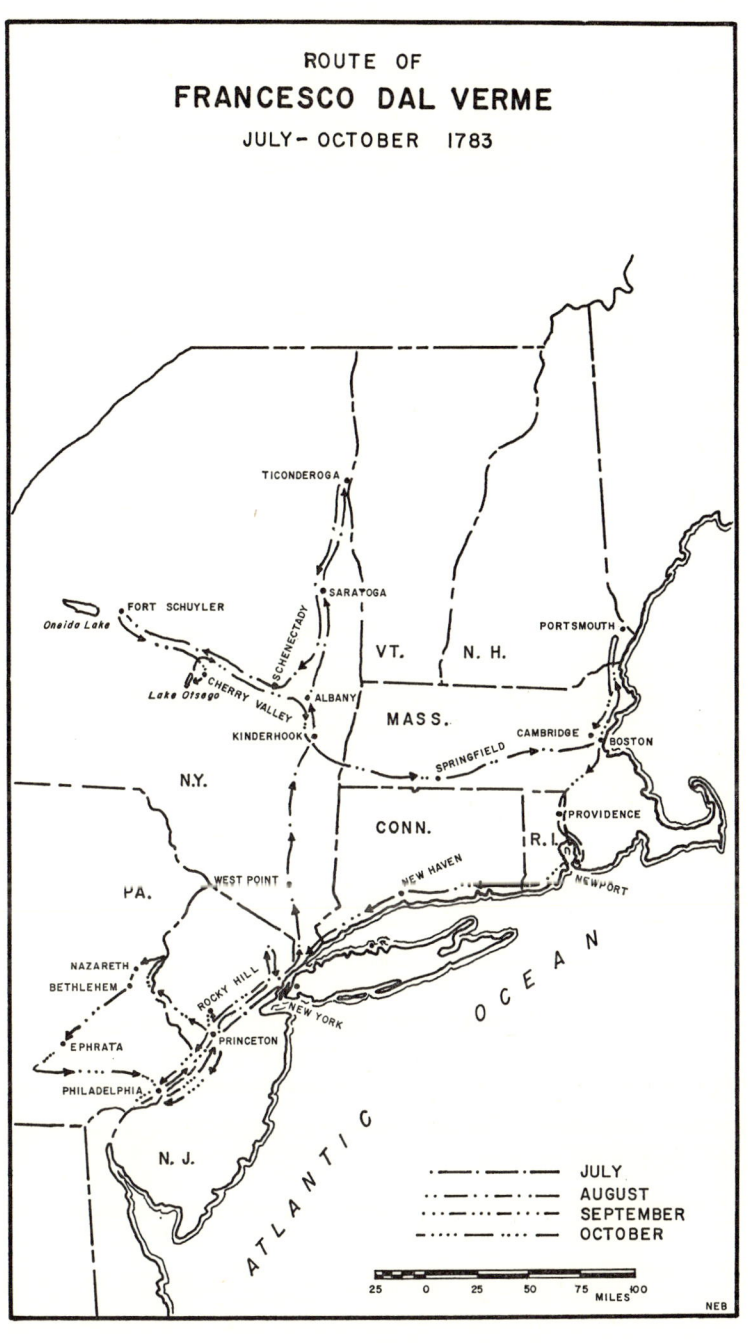

the way. (18 miles.) The place, composed of a few houses clustered around the church, is on the main road to Philadelphia.

July 7. Set off in the diligence. (This is a lumbering four-horse carriage with a top, which may be enclosed; it has room for eighteen, three for each bench.) [16] Changed horses twice; arrived at Princeton (44 miles). (A half guinea per place). Much of the countryside along this road is uncultivated but near the dwelling-houses it is well-tended. (*Town* refers to a village, not to a city.) This place has only a few houses and a college which is now the seat of the Congress of the thirteen United States. Mr. [Elias] Boudinot is now serving as president.[17] I met him following dinner at the tavern with four members of Congress, for two of whom, Mr. [Jacob] Read and Mr. [Ralph] Izard, I had brought letters of introduction from London. Tea. In the evening witnessed fireworks in celebration of the anniversary of Independence.[18] Fair.

July 8. After breakfast with Mr. Read accompanied him to see the College, a large three-story building with twenty-seven windows in front. Congress meets in the Library. There are seventy students, almost two for each room.[19] Upstairs there is the famous clock with planetary movements made in *1738* by Mr. [David] Rittenhouse of Philadelphia; it is not working at present because it was damaged by the English who would have carried it off had they been able to do so.[20] Most of the scientific apparatus was destroyed or taken by the enemy. In the taverns one can still see vessels from the College being used as containers for sugar, tea, flowers, etc.[21] The organ was converted into bullets. Had dinner and tea at the home of the President.[22] Fierce claps of thunder during the night; storm.

July 9. Breakfast with Mr. [Theodorick] Bland, dinner at the tavern. Since the diligence was full, I hired a light buggy-wagon and without changing horses arrived at midnight at Elizabeth (44 miles) (6 dollars). The inn was full, so it was well that the night was short.

July 10. Went by horseback, generally following the Passaic River, to see its falls (23 miles distant). Both sides of the river are very fertile and have many fine homes. The falls are quite like those of Bellano [?], but larger.[23] Since the heat was excessive, the moon was preferable to the sun. Returned in the evening to Elizabeth (23 miles). Fair.

July 11. Went two miles to get the boat for New York where I arrived at dusk. (18 miles.) Dined at the home of Mr. Steward. Downpour.

July 12. Had dinner with Mr. Steward. Wrote to father, Albert, and [sister] Visconti at Milan and enclosed the journal up to June 30, 1783. Light rain.

July 13. Left at two in the afternoon in a merchant shallop for West Point (55 miles above the mouth of the Hudson River) where the American troops are now encamped. Arrived that night at eleven. A guide and the moon led me to the tavern, 190 feet above the river bank. I could not get a bed because all were occupied, nor drinking water because it had rained after dinner. Downpour all night.

July 14. Breakfast in the tent of Baron [Frederick] Steuben, Inspector General of all the American troops. (He is a German and was for many years in the service of the King of Prussia.) Accompanied him around the camp and along the edge of the river where it bends to a near-perfect right angle. During the war the navigation of enemy vessels was obstructed by means of a heavy chain which, stretched across the river, formed an unbreakable barrier for any craft obliged to trim its sails at this point. This move was of very great importance.[24] Dined with Baron Steuben, took tea with *General Worington* [General Jedediah Huntington?], and lodged with General [Henry] Knox.[25] Storm at midday.

July 15. A military parade at seven o'clock; good band. Breakfast with General Knox. At midday left by boat with Baron Steuben and various officers and went upstream to the headquarters of General [George] Washington (7 miles).[26] After reading the letters from the American ministers in London and Paris which I presented to him, the General proposed that I accompany him on a journey he planned to undertake in two days.[27] An account of this will follow. After dinner returned to West Point. Had tea with General [Huntington?]. Frost in the morning. Fair.

July 16. Breakfast with the General and others. Went to General Washington's quarters for dinner where I remained overnight. Family supper at nine o'clock. Fair.

July 17. Breakfast at nine o'clock. At eleven the General's double-teamed carriage was ready to take us on an outing, but an unforeseen development obliged him to remain at home, which left me free to choose a saddle horse instead. Went with two officers to inspect the camp occupied by ten thousand Americans during the previous winter. It lies at the foot of a mountain watered by the Hudson or North River and surrounded by a dense forest which has been cleared at this place into a delightful plain. In the space of five weeks the soldiers built their quarters of logs set in place at right angles and roofed with boards; each cabin could accommodate thirty soldiers. Behind were the officer's quarters and some distance away the hospital and the hall for receiving General Washington's orders of the day.[28] Dinner at two. Tea at seven. Supper at nine. Clear.

July 18. In the morning departed with General Washington, two field officers, and the Governor of the State of New York [George Clinton], in the General's boat of nine oars. Arrived at eight in the evening at Kinderhook (80 miles). There is no tavern here, but American hospitality provided for us well enough. Clear.

July 19. Departed at four o'clock. When we had gone eighteen miles and were four miles from Albany, a canoe came alongside us to deliver a letter to the General inviting him to come ashore where two deputies from the town of Albany were waiting to receive him and offer light refreshments.[29] Had breakfast and arrived at Albany at noon (22 miles). The fort greeted the General with a thirteen-gun salute, and flags were raised both here and at the river bank. All the commonalty and leading townsmen greeted us and accompanied us to the tavern where we partook of a dinner with covers for thirty-two. Instead of fruit they served us tobacco, pipe, brands, and candles, and everyone except the General, me, and two others spent more than two hours alternately parching his throat with smoke and moistening it with wine. Had tea at the home of Mr. [Abraham] Ten Broeck, mayor of the town, which is a fairly large place with houses built in Dutch style.[30] Lodged with General Schuyler, a very rich man, whose home is as magnificent as it is well situated on a hill a quarter of a mile from the city and the same distance from the river, of which it enjoys a panoramic view.[31] Ate supper here with two of his married daughters and an Indian colonel from Canada who spoke French and English fluently in addition to five Indian languages.[32]

July 20. After breakfast set out on horseback with General Schuyler, the Mayor, and others. When we had gone twelve miles we got into a boat and crossed the Mohawk River to see the great falls which are seventy feet in height, a thousand in width.[33] Passed by the place where General [John] Burgoyne first engaged the American forces. Arrived at Saratoga at six in the evening (35 miles). Dinner and lodgings at General Schuyler's house.[34] The road is almost always in the midst of woods, but generally good. Cloudy.

July 21. Saratoga consists of a few houses and many sawmills.[35] Here General Burgoyne and his army surrendered to General [Horatio] Gates. Left by horse and after crossing the Hudson River from east to west, we met more than two hundred persons, among them entire families, who were returning from Indian captivity. (During the recent war two Indian nations supported the American cause, and four, the British.) [36] The girls said that they had suffered no violence and that they all had been generally well treated.[37] The greatest source of distress was the frequent separation of members of the same family. Light refreshments at Fort Edward (14 miles).[38] The Hudson River is navigable to this place. There are two cataracts here, the second one of which has some remarkable petrifications.[39] Arrived in the evening at Fort George, now dismantled (15 miles). Here the boats that had been brought overland from Fort Edward were placed on Lake George.[40] Fishing provided our supper, and we extended our mattresses in a house of only one room in which all the members of the family slept in the same bed. Rain after dinner.

July 22. Left our horses here in the custody of thirty soldiers who had come with us as far as this place. We, thirty-nine persons in all, got into three boats, each one of which carried six armed soldiers who did the rowing. Our provisions consisted of biscuit, beverages, and a live sheep. We counted on our skill as anglers to provide food, and in the course of a fourteen-mile sail we caught enough fish for dinner. Arrived at eight in the evening (36 miles) at the end of this lake and at the entrance of Lake Champlain. (Lake George is also called *Lac Sacrament.*) [41] Slept under the tents. Not one house did we see during the entire day, but we did sight about seventy islands and rocks all covered with very fine trees.

July 23. Breakfasted on fish. Had two botas transported overland (2 miles) to place on Lake Champlain. Went ashore to see Ticonderoga where there are remnants of the English defenses of the War of 1754.[42] We killed a snake here nine feet long and four inches in diameter called a *Ratel-snake,* which has a link of concentric horn rings—in this case six inches long—on the tail with which it makes a great noise. The heat obliged us to go ashore again to cover the boats with branches. Reached Crown Point (18 miles) where some fortifications are still standing.[43] When we were within twenty steps of them a big bear, black as velvet, emerged and fled. We ate in a hut and then turned back in our boats (7 miles). We pitched our tents by the lakeside, but the mosquitoes would not let us sleep although with the help of the wind we had much smoke from our numerous fires.[44]

July 24. Arrived once more (11 miles) at the portage to Lake George (2 miles). Pitched the tents. Breakfast and dinner of fish, as usual. We had left our sheep here for slaughter on our return, but the guards let it graze too far from them and it was carried off by a bear with two cubs which they chased in vain. At five in the afternoon the boats were ready. We reached Lake George in the evening (7 miles). The insects took over the camp until the smoke from the fires built all around us, together with a fresh wind, enabled us to regain possession. During the night an incessant screaming of panthers on the other side of the lake. Very hot.

July 25. Set out at three in the morning; at one in the afternoon we came to an island (18 miles), where we had lunch. A few minutes' downpour drenched us. Our catch of fish was so plentiful that we kept only the best of them. The most common fish is a kind of perch, but in running streams there are also pike and some red trout. On our arrival at Fort George we found bowers lighted by torches of dry wood. (The American troops have a special knack for this type of construction.) [45] Here we met Baron Steuben and his party on their way to Canada.[46] Encamped. In the course of our

Count Antonio and Countess Maria Camilla Taverna dal Verme. (Courtesy of Count Gian Carlo dal Verme)

Major General Philip Schuyler, by John Trumbull. (Courtesy of The New-York Historical Society, New York City)

General George Washington, by Joseph Wright. (Courtesy of The Historical Society of Pennsylvania)

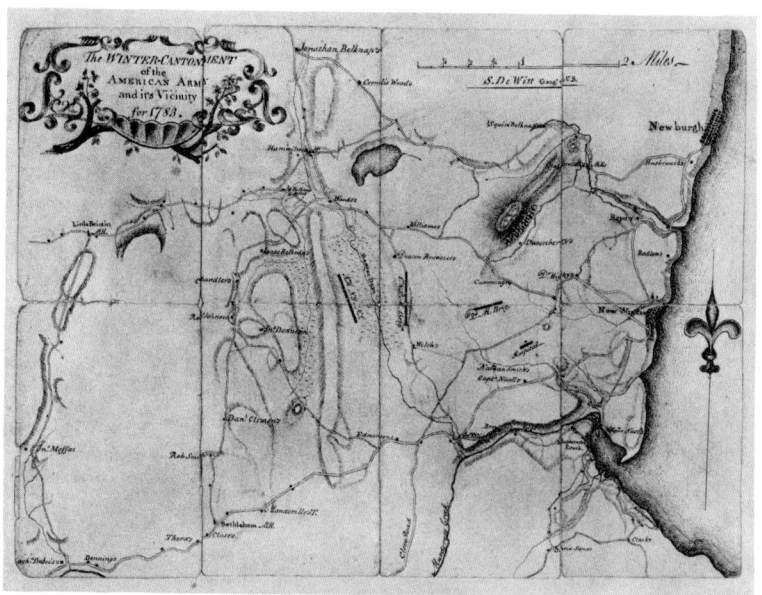

Winter cantonment of the American Army, by Erskine-DeWitt. (Courtesy of The New-York Historical Society)

Indian family, by Baroness Hyde de Neuville. (Courtesy of The New-York Historical Society)

journey we went ashore, most of the time into impenetrable woods, to empty our leaky boats. Saw some bears in the morning. The wind had leveled a great number of trees, many of which, although quite large, lay uprooted on the bare rocks. Clear after dinner.

July 26. After breakfast left for Fort Edward (14 miles), where we watered the horses. At four o'clock in the afternoon we had dinner in Saratoga (15 miles) at the home of General Schuyler. Visited a sawmill in which fifteen saws simultaneously cut a log into sixteen boards. All the buildings at this place except the church were burned by the enemy.[47] Sky overcast.

July 27. Fog so thick that it was impossible to see beyond ten steps. (The local custom is to take antidotes against the ill effects of fog in dosages determined by the density of the fog, which may be of seven grades.[48] Distinction is made between a fog of one, two, and up to seven drafts, by which is meant drafts of whiskey, rum, brandy, etc. Almost everyone in America conforms to this practice with happy results.) After lunch (and proper antidote which upon due consideration we unanimously decided should be of the fifth grade) we arrived at the mineral springs (12 miles).[49] These are three springs whose water is very cold and constantly bubbling. At intervals the water from one of them overflows through a round hole, a palm in diameter, onto a rock three feet high shaped like a cone resting on its base.[50] They told us that ten years ago the rock was not more than two feet high and that its height had been increased by the calcareous substance deposited when the water, which is usually six inches below the opening, overflows. The water has a salty taste and smells of sulphur. Many use it for treating gout, dropsy, and asthma, usually with full recovery when taken locally. It makes excellent bread without yeast and salt. The experiment made for us was entirely successful. The dough rose in less than two minutes—to be exact in 1 minute, 40 seconds, and 52 thirds [52/60 of a second] according to a man who had the watch which marked the seconds (he calculated these last in his head).[51] Although we had a guide we lost our way in the forest and rode twenty instead of twelve miles to get to Colonel [James] Gordon's, where we found a good dinner.[52] This road was terrible, obstructed by trees whose tops were seldom below the clouds and whose breadth was proportionally great. The road is full of holes across which bridges and logs have been laid to permit passage. Had we not gone over it we would have doubted that it could be done. The previous evening we met a man of seventy years who had left his home, ninety miles from Philadelphia, to go to Canada to look for his two daughters who had been captured by the Indians five years before, at which time they had killed his two sons, who were defending themselves, and his wife, who was unable to follow them. The good old man had saved himself by hiding. After dinner we came to within two miles of Schenectady (12 miles). Here two Indians, an ambassador and his interpreter, of the two nations (Oneida and Tuscarora) who supported the Americans, presented to General Washington a letter in the form of a memorial requesting rum, powder, and ammunition for hunting; these supplies they obtained.[53] Thunderstorm, then clear.

July 28. Thick fog. On our way to Fort Rensselaer, we went into a house that had been used as a fort. The commander explained to the General that the small cannon which saluted us did not fire thirteen shots for lack of powder. When we arrived at Fort Rensselaer we received a thirteen-gun salute.[54] The troops presented arms. After maneuvers we dined with the officer corps in a group of twenty-five. The echo in these mountains is very clear. Lodged in a nearby house. Cloudy.

July 29. After breakfast went to see many houses that had been burned and replaced with others constructed of thick beams fortified on all sides.[55] On our arrival at Fort *Aldemar* [Herkimer ?] (31 miles) the troops presented arms and the cannon saluted us. Dinner with twelve officers of the garrison. Visited Fort *Etham* [Dayton ?] (2 miles), and slept in the kitchen of the tavern.[56] Clear.

July 30. Set out at five o'clock. For thirty miles we traveled entirely in the midst of woods over a very bad road. We came to many bridges which seemed safe but were actually unfit for use. Of the first four, two collapsed entirely and two partially, under the weight of the advance horses. We avoided the others.[57] Midway on our route we halted in the ruins of an Indian dwelling to drink some liquor. After dinner we entered a house whose sole occupants were three women and three naked children lying on the ground covered with a bear skin. The men had gone hunting. All of the utensils were made of tree bark except an iron kettle to place on the fire. After a march of twelve hours always under a pelting rain we came to Fort Schuyler, which is totally destroyed.[58] It is located on the Mohawk River. We proceeded another mile to a watercourse which by means of only two lockgates is rendered navigable as far as Lake Oneida, eighteen miles away.[59] Some thirty soldiers who were with us cut bark from the trees and constructed two huts; in the middle of these they built a big fire which dried us out and cooked our dinner. They made our beds from pine needles covered with blankets. Fair in the evening and night.

July 31. Very dense fog and cold. Got into a boat left here on the Mohawk River expressly for us and went downstream (40 miles) to Fort Herkimer, or *Aldemar,* in twelve hours. Met an Indian family which was returing up the river—father, mother, and four children—each one using a paddle to push their bark canoe which might have weighed fifty Milanese pounds. When they were thirty feet from us [the father] shot with his gun two wild ducks which we acquired in exchange for rum. The navigation of this entire river (during the war only the Indians used it) is very difficult at present because of the many trees which obstruct its bed and its surface. Although few tracts of land are under cultivation here, the broad open plains extending from the banks of the river appear to be very fertile. Lodged in the house where we stayed on the 29th. Storm.

August 1. Descended the Mohawk River (6 miles) and came to an extensive fall which obliged us to go four miles overland to get into the boat. The view from both banks here is picturesque. After three more miles ate breakfast with Mr. *Alkemar* [Herkimer?].[60] Landed (13 miles) and dined at the house where we spent the night of the 29th. After dinner rode twelve miles to Cherry Valley where we found plenty of milk, but not beds. The road is fairly good, with an occasional house along it. All the people here are Irish; nevertheless they suffered a great deal during the war.[61] Storm.

August 2. Thunderstorm. Rode fourteen miles through woods and over a bad road to Otsego Lake; here issues the Susquehanna River, which empties into the Chesapeake *river.* Returned by the same road (14 miles) to Cherry Valley in a downpour of rain; had dinner, and arrived in the evening at Canajoharie on the Mohawk River where we dined for the second time. All the local dignitaries were present.[62] Slept here. Clear.

August 3. Proceeded downstream (42 miles) to Schenectady which we reached in eight hours. The city fathers welcomed us and provided a dinner of thirty-two covers. General Washington was also honored here by many Indians, around two hundred in all, from the two nations allied with the Americans. The Indians generally leave their heads uncovered and tie their hair in the middle of the head in such a way that it stands out like a rigid tail; others wear turbans made of black fur. They daub a great deal of rouge of French importation on their olive skin or paint the face half black and half red. Some of them slash the rim of the ear and attach leaden rings to the oblong band of flesh hanging from its two ends; others leave the rim attached to only one end of the ear, and encircle it with bits of lead. Many of them make a large cut in the fleshy part of the ear into which they insert four or five rings. They also insert many of these ornaments into the nasal septum, but usually the rings are of the type worn by our ladies known as *Malabar*. Some Indians wear a high collar as well as bracelets on the upper and lower arm and wrist made of some white metal which they buy as silver. Plates of various sizes, likewise made of this metal, are attached to animal tails and suspended from the back and front of the neck. Some of them wear undergarments and a kind of Indian cassock with tight sleeves, but more frequently their costume consists of a shirt of very thick cloth and a woolen blanket which they wrap around them when it is cold and put over their head when it rains. Their trousers are simply two arm lengths of red or blue cloth, half a yard wide, which they pass between the thighs and over a belt worn at the navel, leaving the two ends of the cloth hanging behind and in front. Their gaiters are made of red or blue cloth sewn so that a fringe about four inches wide runs the length of the gaiters. The color of the fringe is red if the gaiters are blue and vice versa. The gaiters extend from the ankles to the knees. Their shoes are made of animal hide. For a pouch they carry the skin of an animal (grasping it by the head, which is left attached). Glass and ceramic ornaments are widely worn. Some carry a bow (a boy was able to hit a coin half buried in the ground six out of eight tries), but they usually hunt with a gun. A small number speak English. Handsome men are few, and handsome women are even fewer. Women carry their babies strapped to a board which hangs lengthwise on the mother's back and has a piece of wood at the bottom to sustain the weight of the child.[63]

Proceeded sixteen miles overland and arrived at Albany in the evening. A good but very deserted road. Lodged with General Schuyler. Warm.

August 4. Breakfast with Colonel [Marinus] Willett. Received many letters and a passport from General Washington.[64] Accompanied the General and his party to the boat which departed in the midst of cannon smoke for his headquarters seven miles above West Point.[65]

Inspected a number of horses with the intention of buying two of them. Dinner, tea, and supper with General Schuyler, with whom I lodged. Terrible storm.

August 5. Breakfast with Mr. [John] Tayler, with whose assistance I bought two saddle horses, one for thirteen guineas, the other for fourteen. Dinner and tea with Colonel [Morgan] Lewis.[66] Supper at lodgings. Very hot and clear.

August 6. Set off by horse on my journey to Boston. Crossed the Hudson River and dined at Kinderhook (20 miles). A good road as far as Barrington (28 miles) where I spent the night. Mild.

August 7. Crossed a very long truss bridge; dinner at Loudon [Otis] (20 miles). Arrived at Westfield in the evening (20 miles). The entire road covered today is in the midst of woods and very high hills. Very hot.

August 8. Dense fog. Crossed the Connecticut River and came to Springfield (12 miles) where I had dinner.[67] Being centrally located between New York, Boston, and the North, Springfield has a magazine containing 17,000 stands of arms and much ammunition. Came to Palmer in the evening (16 miles), at which time there was a violent windstorm that lasted an hour. Very hot.

August 9. Dinner at Brookfield (16 miles). Spent the night at Worcester (19 miles). Very cold wind, but clear.

August 10. Dinner at Marlboro (16 miles). On entering Weston (17 miles), where I spent the night, a man holding a staff of office stopped me to inquire what pressing business obliged me to travel on that day and threatened, at the same time, to compel me to dismount at the first tavern and also pay a fine of twelve dollars.

(Special laws of Massachusetts, of which Boston is the capital, prohibit traveling on Sunday, but they are not generally enforced at present.) I had already been warned that a tip sufficed to obtain immunity when the laws were in complete operation and virtually nothing now that they have almost lost their effectiveness. In fact, after a comic argument, in less than two minutes I put a half mile between myself and the man, whom I left standing in the middle of the road cursing the entire French nation (to which he thought I belonged) and vowing to get even with the first Frenchman who might come his way.[68] Fair, but very cold.

August 11. Arrived in Boston at eight in the morning (14 miles). The road is good and there are many fine farmhouses along it. (They make a practice here of attaching to walls or poles small painted houses made of wood to entice birds to build their nests in them.) Presented letters to Mr. [James] Bowdoin and to Governor [John] Hancock. With the former had tea and supper and spent the evening. Dined at the tavern's table d'hôte, then took a walk around the port; on a French vessel came upon a twelve-year-old cabin boy from the parish of San Lorenzo in Milan. Rain and fog.

August 12. Breakfast at the tavern's table d'hôte. Spent the morning having the saddles repaired; both being new, they had rubbed calluses in the course of the journey and ruined both the horses. Dined at two with the Governor and guests. After coffee accompanied the French Consul, Mr. [Sieur Philip Joseph de] Lé Tombe, in his carriage for a visit to Dr. [Samuel] Cooper, Lieutenant Governor Mr. [Thomas] Cushing and Mr. [Samuel] Adams.[69] Spent the evening with the Governor. Fog and rain.

August 13. Breakfast as usual. Walked around the city. Boston is situated on a peninsula which slopes toward the sea. This peninsula is connected to the continent by a mere tongue of land which at high tide appears to be only a road; consequently the place could be fortified at very little cost. Nearby is a promontory commanding the entire city. Here they have built a kind of harbor lighthouse on top of which there is a barrel of pitch and tow, ready to be lighted in case of surprise; with such a signal 40,000 armed men can gather in the city in less than twenty-four hours.[70] Charlestown, which was burned by the British on June 17, 1775, during the Battle of Bunker Hill, can be seen from this point.[71] This melancholy sight preserves in the hearts of the Bostonians sentiments of liberty and revenge. Only the Charles River separates Charlestown, situated at the angle formed by the junction of this river with the Mystic, from the peninsula. Once there were many houses [in Charlestown], now there are only a few, and these of recent construction. At present there is talk of building a long bridge, to connect it with Boston, replacing the four ferry boats which are in continuous operation. The port of Boston can accommodate 500 sails, but its entrance is difficult and dangerous, since the sole channel is approximately ninety feet long [wide ?] and very close to the island on which there is the fort equipped with strong batteries.[72] This situation protects the city from attack by sea. Saw an American ship here getting ready to leave for the East Indies. Dinner with the French Consul. Paid some visits and stopped at Mr. [Abiel ?] Smith's where I had tea and supper.[73] *There were six ladies five of them very fines.* A terrible storm forced the company to remain until after midnight. One of the games consisted of proposing in succession *le nom de sa Maitresse* and having all the players find a descriptive word beginning with the initial of the lady designated. One of our beauties came out extremely well. *Quel plaisir étant si loin de son objet, se trouver au milieu de ceux qu'ils en font l'elloge!* Rain.

August 14. Breakfast and dinner as usual at the tavern. Paid some visits in the morning and had tea and supper with Mr. Bowdoin. Fog.

August 15. At dinnertime arrived by a good road to Salem (19 miles), a place famous for the large number of successful shipowners during the war. Went to Marblehead (4 miles) to look at a vast quantity of fish from these coasts and Newfoundland laid out in the sun to dry. Passed by Ipswich, a small but pleasant place, where the innkeeper hails from Casale Monferrato in Italy. Reached Newbury in the evening (23 miles). Clear.

August 16. Crossed the bay, and reached Portsmouth (22 miles) at ten o'clock. The entire road is good and bordered by beautiful fields. Presented a letter to Mr. [Jonathan ?] Warner with whom I dined and afterward went to his house in the country (4 miles).[74] After tea there was another meal where, among other things, I ate for the first time young corn on the cob, which is either boiled in water or roasted over a grate and seasoned with fresh butter, salt, and pepper—a hearty beggar's meal, as someone we know would say. Returned to town. At eight o'clock went to the home of Mr. [John] Langdon to present a letter from General Washington.[75] Here I was on the instant struck by the beauty of Madame whom I saw by the light of a distant candle. Mr. Langdon urged me to stop at his house. Sudden change in plans for the length of my stay here. I had first decided on one day, but my tongue chose three. Had supper, then like a flash of lightning (although it was actually nearly midnight) came the hour which is most painful to *un A . . . . e.* Clear.

August 17. Breakfast with the lady of the house; daylight increased rather than diminished my admiration for her. Went with Mr. Langdon to the Congregational meetinghouse, a large church.[76] It is impossible to describe the beauty of the ladies, or their number, or the elegance of their attire, chiefly fashioned according to the latest French taste. From time to time, as if to enable the minister to catch his breath, four boys and some men sang psalms in counterpoint. Dinner and supper with the hosts. After dinner once more to the church; then paid some visits and had tea at one of the homes. Clear.

August 18. On Monday took a walk around the town, which is small, but has a few fine residences. Dined at home, then visited the dancing school. This is held twice a week; the tuition is three dollars a month. At present there are around sixty pupils. The teacher is fairly good but drunk 168 hours a week. The hall in which four public balls are held each month during the winter is fairly attractive.[77] Had tea and supper at home. (Oh, how short is the day!) Rain.

August 19. Went by boat with Mr. Langdon (3 miles) to the lighthouse at the entrance of the harbor which is spacious and safe. There are a number of forts, and a very large one is being planned.[78] Dinner with Mr. [James] Sheafe, then went on an excursion by carriage with Mr. Langdon (10 miles) and saw a race of their horses.[79] Had tea and supper with Colonel [William] Whipple. With great regret took leave of my hosts. Clear.

August 20. Left Portsmouth at five o'clock and dined at Newbury (22 miles); at five after dinner reached Salem (20 miles) where I had tea and supper with Mr. [William] Wetmore.[80] Clear.

August 21. Dinner at Boston (24 miles) with Mr. [James ?] Sullivan. Tea with Mr. [Isaac] Sears. Paid a visit to Mme. Deblois.[81] Her pretty daughter sang and played the harpsichord divinely. Finished the evening at Dr. [James] Lloyd's where Mademoiselle Hunter of Newport played the piano with a masterly touch and sang in Italian. (Patriotic music performed by a perfect beauty, oh what effect!) [82] Clear.

August 22. Left at nine o'clock with all the town officials, the Governor, French Consul, and others for a visit to Rainsford Island (10 miles) where the smallpox hospital is located.[83] Passed the spot where a French vessel of 74 [tons] sank, but its crew and cannons were saved. The United States of America built one like it in Portsmouth, christened it *The America,* and made a gift of it to the King of France; it set sail in July 1783.[84]

At two in the morning went to see a fire in town. The flames enveloped a stall in which nine horses perished, and reduced to ashes an entire warehouse, another stall, two haylofts, and many small shops. The tide's being low rendered the pumps almost useless. The townsmen organize clubs composed of twenty-five or thirty families, all of whom, when the house of an associate catches on fire, rush to help him. Each member keeps a leather bucket stamped with his name which contains a large canvas sack, and both are immediately dispatched to the scene of a fire. All the houses have an open gallery on the roof, which is made of wood, and when a fire breaks out in town, everyone wets the top and sides of his house to prevent any sparks from setting it on fire.[85] Passed the evening and had supper with Mr. Bowdoin. Clear.

August 23. Breakfast with the French Consul with whom I went to Cambridge. (8[7] miles.) On my return to town dined with Governor Hancock; afterwards went in the French Consul's carriage to take tea with Mr. [James] Swan (4 miles).[86] Spent the evening with Mr. Sears. On Saturday everyone takes an excursion to the country. There are 700 cabriolets in Boston, and since it is joined to the mainland by only an isthmus there is a continuous traffic over this road. Excessively warm.

August 24. Breakfast and dinner with the French Consul, tea and supper with Mr. Smith. Here I met Mr. *Molliere,* a thirty-year-old Swede who speaks Italian quite well.[87] He was in Milan seven years ago and was recommended to Mr. Fanzi. He travels for pleasure. Very hot.

August 25. Breakfast at the house of the French Consul. Sailed with him and a group of twelve ladies, the Governor, Lieutenant Governor, and others to the fort (4 miles), which saluted us with thirteen salvos. This fort, destroyed by the English before their evacuation, is being restored to an excellent state of defense. From here continued by boat with part of the company to the lighthouse one hundred feet high (6 miles). Neptune, irritated by the liberty taken by a venerable patriot in plowing through the waves with a canvas cap instead of a wig, ordered the winds to shift in midcourse the tranquillity of the sea. The elements readily obeyed, and as it usually happens when subordinates and executors of supreme commands spitefully exceed their superiors' orders, they began to amuse themselves by blowing the accursed cap two miles away from its owner, who was left with his pate entirely exposed. The rest of us were also victims, arriving with him at our destination completely drenched by the salty humor which the old man had set in motion.[88] Returned to the fort in a small two-oar felucca, where we had dinner and tea. Supper at the home of Mr. [Samuel] Breck.[89] Very warm in the morning, and very cold in the evening. Rain.

August 26. Breakfast at the tavern. Dinner at the home of [William Cushing], the Chief Justice of the Court which opened today. Tea with Mr. Sears. Dance and supper at the home of the French Consul. Of the sixteen ladies present, only four were not beautiful. Cold.

August 27. Went to Cambridge (3½ miles) and had breakfast with Mr. [Nathaniel] Tracy.[90] Returned to the city and dined with Mr. Cushing, Lieutenant Governor. Tea at the home of Mr. [John ?] Livingston. Spent the evening and took supper with Mr. Sears. Temperate.

August 28. Went to the dancing school, where more than eighty girls and many boys were in attendance. (The fee is four dollars a month, and six dollars at entrance.) Lessons are given twice a week. Dinner with Mr. Breck. Spent the evening at the home of Dr.

Lloyd, where Mademoiselle Hunter, whom I have already mentioned, entertained the company with music. Wrote a letter to Father. Dinner, tea, and supper with a number of ladies at the home of the French Consul. Clear.

August 29. [No entry.]

August 30. Went to Cambridge (3½ miles), and in company with Mr. Tracy visited Bunker and Prospect Hills, where in the course of one day the English lost 1,500 soldiers and 92 officers while the Americans lost only 300. Saw the University of Cambridge [Harvard], which has a fine library of 12,000 volumes. There are 164 students who pay thirty guineas a year for complete maintenance. Dinner at the home of Mr. Tracy. After returning to Boston, took supper with Mr. Sears.

August 31. Went (5 miles) with Mr. Breck to see a beautiful estate, the home of Mr. [Benjamin] Hitchbourn, who married the widow of his superior, whom he had accidentally killed with a pistol.[91] Dinner with the French Consul; tea and supper with Mr. Smith. Storm.

September 1. Breakfast with Mr. Sears. Spent the morning with Miss Hunter. In the evening went to Wrentham [?] (27 miles). Ten miles from Boston the land begins to be uncultivated. Cold.

September 2. At eleven o'clock arrived at Providence (18 miles). It is a small town washed in the middle by an arm of the sea; a frigate can enter within a mile of the place. Dinner at the tavern. Took tea and spent the evening at the home of Mr. [Jabez] Bowen, Deputy Governor.[92] Cold.

September 3. In company with the French Consul, who rejoined me, went to visit the College [of Rhode Island], which is large but has only a few students because it was closed during the war. From here walked in procession with the town officials to a large, fine church where the candidates for degrees stood on a platform and the President in the pulpit. Orations on a variety of topics were delivered. Good vocal music.[93] Dinner and tea at the home of Mr. Bowen. Supper with a group at the tavern. Cold.

September 4. Visited some French vessels, accompanied by Mr. Lamfrey [?], the royal commissioner, at whose home dined together with the French Consul. In the morning attended a small concert at Mr. [Samuel] Chace's.[94] Took tea with Mr. [Moses] Brown, the richest man in the town; in the evening danced with his daughter, the ugliest creature in the universe.[95] When the students receive their degrees there is always a dance and supper in the evening, for which they pay thirty *soldi,* our money. Around sixty ladies and many men were in attendance.[96] Temperate.

September 5. Set off with the French Consul for Newport.[97] Passed the harbor and by a fairly good road reached Warren in time for dinner (12 miles). Six miles beyond we crossed a strait of one and one-half miles in seven minutes and reached Rhode Island. On arrival at Newport (11 miles) paid a visit to Mr. [Christopher] Champlin and to the Hunter family.[98] Everything pleasant. Supper at the tavern. Strong wind and cold.

September 6. Went (5 miles) to pay a visit to the nephew of General Washington.[99] This island is fourteen miles long and three miles wide. It was once the garden spot of these people, but now all the trees including fruit trees and shade trees are gone, cut by the enemy.[100] Dinner at the tavern, then to the Synagogue, where there were one hundred Hebrews, and to the Anabaptist Church.[101] Visited the Champlin, [Benjamin] Brenton, and Hunter homes, at the last of which stayed for tea.[102] Excellent weather.

September 7. Crossed a bay (3 miles), Conanicut Island, one mile wide, another bay (3 miles), and arrived at Charlestown on the mainland for dinner (18 miles); Barber's Tavern in the evening (23 miles). The road is very bad and quite steep. Near here there is a fort whose garrison was massacred by the English following its surrender.[103] The anniversary of this event was commemorated yesterday and the preacher omitted nothing which might sustain the public animus against such cruel enemies. A few days ago an entire house with a forty by thirty foot frontage was transported a mile by land and six by water.

September 8. Covered four miles and came to an inlet (1 mile) on the other side of which is New London, much of it burned.[104]

Breakfast and dinner at Lyme (10 miles). Crossed the mouth of the Connecticut River and arrived in the evening at *Killing's* [Killingworth?] (15 miles), where there are many Acadian families who, although neutral, were transported here by the English in 1749.[105] Very bad road. Clear.

September 9. Came to Guilford in a downpour of rain (10 miles). Breakfast and with good weather arrived at New Haven within an hour. (18 miles.) Dinner at the tavern. Visited the President of the College.[106] In the evening the College windows were illuminated from within by affixing the candles to a hilt which served as a candlestick. After one year the freshmen become second-year men, and on the eve of graduation they are obliged to run in their night clothes, each one carrying a long stick, for more than thirty minutes about the college yard and in and out of the chapel striking the benches with the sticks. They are followed, or more precisely are joined periodically, by fiddlers and jugglers similar to our Calabrians. More than sixty young men took part in the race, which was executed at such speed that it would have been dangerous to have got in their way.[107] Some persons were on the bell tower blowing little trumpets. After fireworks and many rockets, every room of any size was converted into a ballroom; a violin in one, a small trumpet in another, and even a lone drum in another sufficed to set in motion the legs of these people so passionately fond of dancing.[108] Temperate.

September 10. At ten o'clock went to the College; from there we went in procession – the professors preceded by the students, candidates for degrees, and the President, in toga and holding a staff – to the church for a program of vocal music and various orations. Dined with the President. Returned to the same church in the same good order as in the morning and heard a debate on whether it is advantageous or not to expel the Loyalists, who number around 25,000 and are rich; the argument was predominately in favor of the affirmative. In the evening there was a public ball in a large hall with more than 140 ladies in attendance.[109] Supper. Clear but very cold.

September 11. Took leave of the French Consul, and came to Stratford at dinnertime (23 miles); arrived at Stamford in the evening (22 miles). Clear.

September 12. (11 miles.) Dinner; proceeded until evening (14 miles). Clear.

September 13. Arrived at Kingsbridge (4 miles), where I received permission to pass from the two guards and came to New York (14 miles). This island is very narrow. Dinner at the tavern. Tea at the home of Mr. Steward. Clear.

September 14. At the post I got a letter from [sister] Visconti written on May 10 and one from Albert of May 8; wrote to Father. Had dinner and tea with Mr. Steward. Rain.

September 15. Dinner at the tavern. Tea with Mr. Steward. Strong wind from the south.

September 16. Set out at six o'clock and arrived at Elizabeth at nine (13 miles). Consigned my trunk at the office of the diligence for shipment to Philadelphia. Continued until evening (26 miles). Strong wind from NW.

September 17. Arrived at Princeton (12 miles) for breakfast. Went to Rocky Hill (5 miles), where General Washington is staying.[110] Had dinner and tea with him. The General does not have a vote in Congress, but his influence is very great and his advice is much sought. Wind.

September 18. Breakfast with the President of Congress. Went to Rocky Hill and returned with General Washington for dinner and tea with Mr. [Richard] Beresford, a delegate from *North* [South] Carolina, who is living two miles from Princeton. (12 miles.) Very warm.

September 19. Breakfast at Trenton (12 miles), a small town. Here General Washington captured 1,400 Germans in 1776. Crossed the Delaware which is navigable and subject to tide up to here, a distance of 190 miles from the sea. Had dinner (3 miles). Arrived at Philadelphia (17 miles). The road is good; in the morning the dust was unbearable and in the afternoon and evening there was a deluge. Rain.

September 20. Breakfast at the common table. Went to fetch my baggage from the stagecoach office. Dinner at the tavern, table d'hôte with two services. Had tea with Baron Steuben (3 miles). Cold and windy.

September 21. Received a note from the Minister of France, M. the Chevalier de la Luzerne, inviting me to stay at his residence.[111] Had my trunk sent there and placed in the house. (Left the horses at the inn.) At ten went to the Quaker meetinghouse where fortunately after half an hour someone rose to his feet, removed his hat from his head, and began uttering three or four words a minute. Then becoming more inspired and altering his voice as if chanting (and becoming increasingly unintelligible even to the Quakers), he went on for three-quarters of an hour exhorting purity of conscience. After an interval, another man kneeled (while the people, hats over their eyes, rose) and prayed for four minutes. Then a third briefly advised them not to scatter while going home, and in less than two hours everything was over. The Holy Spirit does not always condescend to move them, in which case the meeting passes in perfect silence. Women are seated on the right, men on the left. Went to the home of Baron Steuben for dinner, 2½ miles (5 miles). Spent the evening at the home of Mr. [Robert ?] Morris.[112] Wind from the west.

September 22. Breakfast at home (that is, with the Minister of France) at ten o'clock, with hot food and wines; this takes the place of supper. Dinner at five o'clock, with only one service. During the morning visited the prisons [113] and from there went to the encampment (2 miles), which contains 1,500 armed troops. Here were read the sentences of death for two sergeants and of one hundred lashes for five soldiers, leaders in the June revolt to obtain pay from Congress at Philadelphia. The two who were to die had already knelt, their eyes bandaged, near the recently prepared grave, with the coffin beside them, and the firing squad with loaded guns had already advanced, when a full pardon was announced for the condemned as well as for the five soldiers. With the same nonchalance which they had shown in meeting death, they rose and after kissing the coat of General [Robert] Howe, who was in command, mounted horses and galloped off to the city.[114] The wife of one of the two sergeants, who was present, was mournful before the pardon and very sorry after it (for she had already made all arrangements for a new marriage). Spent the evening in paying visits. Clear.

September 23. Set off with my horses and arrived at Princeton (44 miles) at dinnertime. After dinner went to the College, where the freshman class was examined. Took supper with Mr. Bland. Cloudy.

September 24. Breakfast with Mrs. [Theodorick] Bland. General Washington introduced me to the President [John Witherspoon] and other members of the College, with whom I went in procession to the church. For five hours we heard orations, among them one stressing music as conducive to the shaping of a great mind, endowed with which man can accomplish anything. Dined with the President of the College, at which time General Washington presented 50 guineas for repairing the college apparatus. Dancing in the evening, but the ballroom was too small.[115] Clear.

September 25. Breakfast at the tavern. Went to Rocky Hill to dine with General Washington, who gave me ten letters for [friends] in Maryland and Virginia. Returned to Princeton in the evening. Rain.

September 26. Set out with Mr. Smith for Easton, where we arrived in the evening (48 miles).[116] Bad and very hilly road. Cloudy.

September 27. Traded one of my horses (because it did not ride well) plus 5 guineas for a four-year-old mare which Mr. Smith had mounted the previous day. The purchase of such a fine animal obliges me to give a description of its native place. Easton is in Pennsylvania on a kind of peninsula six miles around, watered by the Delaware, by another river [Lehigh], and by a small brook. Although it is situated on an elevation, its being entirely surrounded by hills makes it extremely warm in the summer and the opposite in winter. The houses, few in number, are made of stone, and for the most part are inhabited by Germans. Dinner at the tavern and tea at the home of Colonel [Neigal] Gray.[117] Rain during the morning.

September 28. Went to Belvidere (14 miles), the estate of Mr. [Robert] Hoops, for dinner;[118] afterwards went squirrel hunting.[119] The dogs treed the animals and we took eight of them with a rifle loaded with ball, since the lofty trees were beyond the reach of shot. These animals abound here; they have cartilaginous wings, similar

A view of Boston, 1779, from the *Atlantic Neptune*, 1780. (Courtesy of the Barre Publishing Co., Barre, Massachusetts)

Yale College and the College Chapel, 1786. (Courtesy of Yale University Library)

to those of bats, which they spread when making a descent. For supper we had a fricassee of our catch whose flavor is good, but not like that of a fowl, as the local people say. Slept here. Belvidere would merit such a name if it were situated on one of the hills which surround it. Clear.

September 29. Breakfast with Mr. Hoops. Crossed the Delaware in a canoe; we had to go and get the boat ourselves there being only an old lady and a girl to attend us, or rather, to take our money. We arrived at Nazareth (14 miles), a settlement of around two hundred Moravians. All the houses are made of stone; water is carried by underground pipes into pumps from which it is obtained by merely turning a jet of water. Service at the tavern is excellent.[120] Local beer is made from molasses. Reached Bethlehem in the evening (10 miles). The road, most of which is through woods, is almost covered with pheasants similar to ours except that the males do not have long tail feathers.[121] Took a walk with Mr. Gokley [Bokley?].[122] (Bethlehem is the leading one of the six Moravian settlements in America.) In the evening went to the church where everybody gathers. They sing accompanied by the organ, violin, viola, violincello, and flute.[123] The sermon was given in German, and they read a list of their missionaries in the East and West Indies, Europe, Africa, and America.[124] There were 140 men and 200 women present. The latter cut their hair and cover their heads with a white cap that has a starched bill and earlaps, like those worn by our Reverend Mothers; over this they wear a fillet of transparent white veil tied in the back.[125] With such uniformity of headdress it is no more possible to make any great distinction among them than among a regiment of soldiers. Their habit is a kind of cloak. The men dress as we do. Clear.

September 30. Breakfast at the tavern which the Society owns and rents to a man who fixes all charges. A lodger gets three meals a day for twenty *soldi* our money.[126] Went with Mr. Gokley to the stable of the lessee of the Society; there were 80 cows and 26 horses (they do not use oxen).[127] Went down to the springhouse where the milk crocks are kept in a container through which water flows constantly. The house for single men, of whom there are 60 at present, is large, with fine dormitories; the chapel has an organ.[128] At the tannery, instead of gallnut they use bark which has been pulverized through a mill like those we use for making gunpowder;

but the hides must be left about 20 months in the tanning liquid, turning them four or six times. On to where they make nails; to the press for extracting flaxseed oil; to the flour mill; to the fullery where they prepare cloth; to the sadler's shop, the shoemaker's, the tailor's; all these, as well as the apothecary's shop and the oven, belong to the Society.[129] Then to the house of the single women of whom there are 100. They make very fine tambour embroidery consisting mostly of trifles to give to women. Succumbing to the custom of buying something, which everyone does who visits this place, I found nothing better than a pair of cotton gloves. Ah, that even while traveling in the New World, one should find himself when he least expects it, constrained to make some unexpected and unusual expenditures! [130] It is prohibited to enter the house of young girls under eighteen. I saw them in the morning at church, together with the boys, 40 of the former, 36 of the latter. The girls dress exactly like the women, of whom only two could have been called beautiful; the same is true of the single women. They lead a sedentary, solitary, restricted life, an unhappy and brief life.[131] Water is supplied to every home by means of a mill which forces it up to a watertower.[132] Persons who hold land own it. The land of the Society is for public use. If a man needs capital to start a trade it is made available by the Society, which supervises the way it is used. If one of the brethren wishes to marry he so informs his superior, who, being acquainted with the petitioner's character and profession, asks the head of the single women which one of her group would be a suitable mate; if the first person proposed does not please the young man, another one is suggested. As a rule now the young man proposes the object of his heart's desire, and if there is no strong reason for opposing the match, he obtains her.[133] Occasionally someone is denied matrimony, and for continuing bad conduct may be expelled from the Society. This sect, which was founded in this century by Count [Nicolaus Ludwig von] Zinzendorf, is especially well suited for America since its members excel in the cultivation of land and the mechanical arts.[134] Dined at the tavern, then visited the boys' chapel where there was a fine recitation. Tea at the home of Mr. Gokley. Went to church in the evening and heard music as usual. Clear.

October 1. Crossed the Schuylkill River, lunch (14 miles); arrived at Reading in the evening (27 miles). Rain and fog.

The Middle States and New England 33

October 2. Passed Reading, a large village surrounded by mountains (18 miles) to go to Ephrata. There are some houses here inhabited by a sect established in 1730 by a certain Conrad Beissel, a German who came to America as a hermit and lived for a few years in solitude until he was induced by his proselytes to come and live among them on the site that has now been developed. They take two vows, chastity and poverty; I do not know whether they occasionally dispense with the former one, but it is certainly impossible for them to renounce the latter, since they have only a small amount of land which provides them with a very frugal table. All matters are resolved by common consent. They do not have a superintendent, but the priest has more influence than anyone else. The men who have taken vows live like monks in a special house; the women have their own house. They can dissolve their vows whenever they wish to leave this community. There have been as many as 60 women and 30 men in this religious order, but now the former number only 25 and the latter 12. The men's habit consists of a long garment of white cotton fustian for summer and of serge worn with a white scapular for winter.[135] They wear a beard. The women have a uniform dress and cut their hair. It is their custom to get up at midnight to sing in counterpoint.[136] They manufacture and sell paper and print in excellent type books for their own use. At the beginning of the war the American troops removed from the convent two wagonloads of paper which they needed for making cartridges.[137] On attaining maturity these people are baptized by immersion up to the neck in a stream; when they emerge they are careful to move in a straight line. To safeguard themselves against carnal temptation the women plunge into cold water during their periods; after doing this a few times they subvert nature to such an extent that two out of three die, and the third one remains an invalid. I noticed that they were generally sallow and so swollen that I would have thought them pregnant had the Priest not assured me that such practice renders a woman sterile even if she should enjoy the pleasures of love, this being the sole reason, given by their enemies, for adopting the custom.[138] Their cells are similar to those of our Capuchins, but perhaps less fetid.[139] There are many families of this sect in the surrounding neighborhood; the men, although married, wear a beard. I forgot to inquire what pleasure an unshaven chin affords in the darkness of the night, but I believe that it is not hard to get this information even in my country. On the evening of the ninth of this month the sect celebrates the washing of feet and the Apostles' supper and serves a meal to everyone present. When I presented myself to the Head, or Priest ([John] Peter Miller, 74 years old), to seek permission to see the interior of their houses I was asked what good that would be to me.[140] After making an indirect reply to this unexpected question I casually directed the conversation toward General Washington. When I showed the General's passport (the only time I had need of it), [Miller] invited me to see everything, to sleep in his cell, and to have supper with him. The meal consisted of a little salt meat served on an earthern plate and coffee.[141] Our companion at table was his secretary, the shoemaker of the convent. At midnight I accompanied them to church where there were only five people. One of them sang quite well, but the others worse than our Cathedral singers on weekdays. Clear.

October 3. Took leave of the convent and went to Lititz (6 miles), another community of monks. Visited their houses and found them to be like the others already mentioned. There were forty-five single men.[142] The host spoke good Italian, having worked as a confectioner in Verona for six years. Breakfasted here. Went to Mr. [Robert] Coleman's furnace (6 miles). Took dinner with the ironmasters and visited the foundry where many stoves and chimneys are cast. In the evening visited the furnace of Mr. Curtis Grubb (8 miles) at whose home I had supper and spent the night. Casting is done twice daily.[143] The mine, which is just under the surface of the ground, renders more than two-thirds [of the ore]. Many cannons were made here. Clear.

October 4. Visited other mines in the morning, one of them rich in copper, but they do not utilize it. Caught some weasels, among them two which had been castrated by others of this breed. This is how it happens: when a male is caught by one more strong than he using his favorite he seeks help from another and together with the females they bite off the testicles of the poor wretch. Of the truth of this I have the assurance of those who have seen it happen. Had dinner here and arrived in the evening at Manheim (10 miles) where I spent the night. Clear.

October 5. Reached Lancaster (10 miles). Attended the Catholic church, which has an organ; the sermon is given in English and

German.¹⁴⁴ Took dinner at the tavern. In the afternoon went to the Lutheran church, where there is a famous organ constructed in Lititz.¹⁴⁵ At the home of Mr. [William] Henry saw a machine which moves against the wind and the current of a stream, but it appears to me impossible to make any use of it.¹⁴⁶ Had tea and spent the evening here. Clear.

October 6. Breakfast at the home of Mr. [Gotthilf Henry Ernest] Mühlenberg, Lutheran minister, who has a small collection of local plants of every kind.¹⁴⁷ Lancaster is very well constructed with regular streets; it contains around six hundred houses. Continued until evening (32 miles). The road is bad, as has generally been the case in the past six days. Clear.

October 7. Arrived at dinnertime in Philadelphia (34 miles). Took up my lodgings with the Minister of France. Had tea and spent the evening at the home of Mr. Morris. Cloudy and cold.

October 8. Breakfast as usual with others. Dinner and tea at Mr. Morris's. Furious windstorm and rain.

October 9. Breakfast and dinner as usual. Attended a concert in the evening, the price of admission 10 *paoli*. Some of the performers were competent, but the music was too difficult for most of them. One of them played a flute concerto; good finger action, poor embouchure. Many ladies, fewer men.¹⁴⁸ Wind.

October 10. Breakfast at the house where a dinner party was held; among the many ladies present was the wife of General Washington.¹⁴⁹ Spent the evening at the home of the President of the state [John Dickinson]. Clear.

October 11. Went (10 miles) to visit Mr. [William] Bartram, a botanist whose father corresponded with the best botanists in Europe, in particular Linnaeus. The garden is luxuriant.¹⁵⁰ Dinner at home. Called on Mrs. Stewart¹⁵¹ and accompanied her for tea and an evening visit with Mr. Dickinson. Variable.

October 12. Breakfast at the house, where mass was celebrated. The Dutch Minister, Mr. [Peter John] Van Berckel, arrived yesterday from Amsterdam after a crossing of 111 days on a vessel of

64 tons. With it was one of 54 tons which is probably lost and a frigate of 32 tons.[152] Saw Mr. [Charles Willson] Peale's collection of paintings. His portrayal of the physiognomy is good, but his coloring is bad and not permanent.[153] Dinner at the house. Tea with Mr. Morris.

October 13. Went out horseback riding. Dined at home. Cold wind.

October 14. Attended a public election. A year's residence in Pennsylvania qualifies one for voting. As in all other countries the rich are more influential than others.[154] Dined at home and spent the evening with Mrs. Bland. Clear.

October 15. Called on the Dutch Minister. Saw the remaining porcelain factory in Philadelphia. The mill for pulverizing the materials is most ingenious. A single horse performs all the operations. The firing is not yet completed. Probably in a country where daily wages are so high the proprietor will bankrupt himself and the manager (both French) will run away! [155] Dinner with the President of the state. Clear.

October 16. Went out riding. Dinner and tea at the home of Mr. Morris where I spent the evening. Clear.

October 17. Visited a small museum (admission one-half French *scudo*) consisting mostly of arms and Indian costumes.[156] Dinner party at the French Minister's house. Spent the evening with Mrs. House [?]. Clear.

October 18. Excursion to Chester (15 miles). Dinner on board the Dutch vessel of 64 tons in which the Minister arrived. The entire ship was in perfect order; 500 men were on board. Returned to Philadelphia (15 miles). Rain after dinner.

October 19. Heard mass at home. Took dinner and spent the evening at the home of Mrs. House. Wind and rain.

October 20. Left in the public conveyance for Princeton (44 miles). Here I rented a horse and rode to General Washington's quarters for dinner (5 miles). In the evening returned to Princeton

(5 miles) and went to the home of the President of Congress. Clear.

October 21. Breakfast with the President of Congress. At midday set off in the diligence for Philadelphia (44 miles). Arrived at seven in the evening which I spent with Mrs. House. Clear.

October 22. Dinner at the home of the President of the state. Passed the evening with Mr. [Samuel] Vaughan.[157] Clear.

October 23. Dinner with Mr. Morris. Went to a public concert in the evening.[158] Good music. Wind.

October 24. Went to the bank to exchange some of the bank's bills and was immediately offered payment in the kind of money I wanted.[159] Had dinner and spent the evening hearing music at the home of Mr. Vaughan. Clear.

New York, July 12, 1783

My dearest Father:
The longer you will have been waiting for this letter, the greater, I am sure, will be the pleasure you will derive from the good news it conveys regarding my health and that of my servant, my successful voyage, and the promising start of my journey by land.

This is the first packet to sail from here since my arrival; it will depart tomorrow. Except for wind recordings, which would be of no interest to us, the enclosed log is like the one which the Captain is delivering to the Postal Office. Although I left Falmouth on May 14, the log starts on the 15th, since on the sea the time of day is reckoned twelve hours in advance.[160] We arrived in port on June 30 at seven in the evening. [During the voyage] the weather was generally good, and the heat did not bother me. I was sick on the second day out and upset two other times.

The ship's company was excellent, though not numerous; a fairly good library which I found on board made the hours seem like minutes. The ship was one of the cleanest (the good order found on English vessels is indescribable) and best ventilated I have ever seen. The fare was abundant and included fresh meat for the first twenty days and plenty of fowl for the remainder of the time. I don't believe I ate a pound of salt meat [during the entire voyage]. There was no want of beer or wine. Tea was served in the morning with small fresh rolls, and excellent coffee after dinner.

Although one feels the heat in [New York], a Lombard, especially one who has spent an occasional summer in Rome, is no stranger to it. This city, part of which has not yet been rebuilt, is now very crowded with many Hessian as well as English troops, and very many Loyalist refugees. The last are leaving daily for either Nova Scotia or Europe. When all these people depart, New York will momentarily be left with few inhabitants.

New York is the only city held by the English; however, they also control Long Island, Staten Island, and a point on the mainland. The above troops do not exceed 25,000 or 30,000 men; it does not appear that they are evacuating these places although there are more than one hundred transport ships and twenty war vessels in this port.

I did not have any letters for the commandant of this place because at the time of my departure from London it was held for certain that the English would have left New York by the time of my arrival there. However, through letters I had for leading citizens and the heads of the thirteen United States, I succeeded in getting myself introduced to him.

I can only congratulate myself most heartily for the courtesies extended to me by those for whom I had letters, particularly one Mr. Steward, the father of a young man who was at Hampstead, England, at the same time I was.

Although I have traveled only 65 miles on the mainland (New York is on the island of the same name and is connected to the continent by a bridge), namely, to *Princetown* or *Princeton* on the road to Philadelphia, 40 miles away, I have already accomplished a good deal, since Princeton is the seat of Congress. Through letters I brought with me from *Doctor* [Benjamin] *Franklin,* the American ambassador to Paris, *Doctor* [William] *Franklin* now in London, and the American plenipotentiaries in London and Paris, Messieurs [Henry] Laurens and [John] Adams, I have met the members and President of Congress, who seem to be most respectable persons. And I shall always be satisfied with the very cordial and hospitable manner in which I have been received.

Princeton is very small. There are two fairly good taverns and a well-built college with seventy students and excellent instructors, so I have been told. During my brief stay there I did not have time for a glass of water at my quarters. One day I dined with the President in a company of thirteen. During the evening there were fireworks to commemorate the anniversary of the Declaration of Independence; in the middle of the celebration they displayed the two initials of the United States. Bad weather had prevented the discharge of the fireworks on the fourth of this month.

Since June 26, Congress has been meeting in Princeton because on the 22nd of that month 200 armed soldiers invaded Philadelphia, then the seat of Congress, to demand their pay. (Nearly all the troops had been furloughed and given, in lieu of pay, bills of credit acceptable only in payment of taxes, and then for only one-eighths of the amount owed, specie payment being required for the rest.) The soldiers obtained only one month's pay, and this, too, in bills which are exchanged for specie at a discount of 60 to 100 per cent. Still, the troops left fairly well satisfied. Several officers were arrested and will be tried.

Congress decided to transfer its seat to Princeton in New Jersey because this province is more disposed than any other to defend Congress in case of mutiny. The situation has become so quiet now that there is not even a picket in the town.

Some of the roads are good. The countryside that is cultivated is very beautiful, but woods and unimproved fields are common.

The cost of living is high in New York (almost as high as in London) because of the above-mentioned population, but on the mainland it is comparable to ours.[161] New York is a large city (almost the size of Pavia). It is well built, yet it contains many houses made of wood including the roof. It has a fairly good theatre which is now open three times a week. Being surrounded by water on three sides, the city could not be better situated for commerce. One has only to look at a map to see how many parts of the interior are accessible by water.

Tomorrow I shall travel sixty miles to present the letters I have for General Washington. On my return here I shall go to Boston, and from there to Philadelphia.

This letter will probably reach you toward the end of next month, since the voyage from here to Europe is of much shorter duration than from there to here. Two days before I left Falmouth the New York packet arrived in twenty-five days, and two years ago in winter another one arrived in sixteen.

I shall certainly have occasion to write you again during the coming month.

I beg your lordship to extend my respects to Mama, to whom I am not writing in order to avoid repetition of letters, and assure her of my most sincere filial regards. I should also like for you to extend my regards to the Tavernas, Giulinis, Visconti, everyone at home, the aunts at Voghera, and all who might inquire of me, particularly Don Apollonio Casati, and, if the occasion should arise, to Marquise Villani and Colonel Colli whom I especially came to know in Paris.

I hope that you and everyone at home are in as excellent health as I am.

With filial love and respect, I kiss your hand and remain, my lord and dearest father,

      Your most obliging and affectionate son,

      Francesco dal Verme

[Enclosed log (see pp. 5–6) endorsed]

August 26, 1783

Boston, August 29, 1783

Dearest Father:
I heard this morning that a vessel is sailing for London with the first favorable wind; consequently I am taking advantage of this occasion to assure you that I and my servant have consistently been enjoying the most perfect health. Time does not allow me to send you a copy of my journal, but this letter contains enough news to afford you much pleasure. I hope that [by now] you will have received my letter of July 12, at which time I also wrote to [sister] Visconti and Alberto Litta.

I left New York on July 6 and arrived at Princeton, the seat of Congress (40 miles), the following day in the stagecoach. On July 11, I returned to New York. On the 13th I sailed up the Hudson River (55 miles) and reached the American camp in the evening. On the 16th [15th] I went to visit General Washington (7 miles), where I remained for the night. On the 18th I left with him and some others for a tour to Lake Champlain, southeast of the Saint Lawrence River, and to within 40 miles of Lake Ontario.

The purpose of this trip was to inspect the posts which need to be fortified. We returned to Albany on August 3; General Washington departed from there on the 4th and I on the 6th, after having bought two saddle horses. I reached Boston on the morning of the 11th (198 miles—there are 62 miles to a degree), left Boston on the 15th, and arrived at Portsmouth the following day (60 miles). I returned to Boston on the 21st, where I shall remain until Monday of next week, at which time I plan to set off for New York (260 miles). I left my baggage and letters of credit in New York while I visited General Washington. I find it more pleasant and convenient to travel by horse than by carriage; consequently I shall have my trunk sent by public conveyance. On my arrival in New York I hope to find letters from you since I know that the June packet has reached that port.

Wasteland, unhealthy climate, poor people, ragged clothing—such is approximately the general idea of this continent in Europe.

But oh how far from the truth is this! The land requires too little work to remain uncultivated; the robustness of the men, the fine color of the women attest the salubriousness of the climate; not only the abundance, but also the luxury in which people live belies their reputed poverty. And the pleasure which everyone who is introduced to their society experiences is incontestable evidence of their gracious manner of living. The peasant does not know what misery is; he eats meat four times a day and drinks tea twice a day. If money is scarce, everything is cheap. At present such is the competition here among ships from Europe (where perhaps they imagined that the Americans were all naked) that they are obliged to sell their merchandise at a loss. The quantity of all kinds of lumber, fish, oil, blubber, material for soap, flour, and salt meat will, before long, bring to this continent enough money to enable it to be recognized as a wealthy country.

The commercial treaty and the definitive treaty of peace have not yet arrived, but orders and vessels have been received for the transport of troops and Loyalists to whom many of the Thirteen States refuse permission to remain. The evacuation is scheduled for next October. The English name will always be detested here, as this war was conducted with incredible cruelty.

On arrival in New York, from where I shall go immediately to Philadelphia, I expect to forward my journal to you by means of the packet. At present I assure you that nothing is of greater concern to me than your good health, and that of Mama and others to whom please extend my respects. I kiss your hand and remain, my lord and dearest father,

      Your most obliging and affectionate son,
      Francesco dal Verme

New York, September 13, 1783

Dearest Father:
I arrived here safe this morning from Boston, which I left on the first of this month. En route, a distance of only 298 miles, I stopped in three towns—Providence, Newport, and New Haven.

I went immediately to the post office where I found two letters, one from [sister] Visconti, dated May 10, and one from Albert, dated May 8.

In reply to my inquiry concerning immediate departures for Europe, I was told that there is a ship sailing this afternoon, so I take this opportunity to tell you how very happy I am that your lordship, Mama, and others are well, as is the case with my servant and me.

I hope that by now you will have received my letter of August 29 from Boston, in which I informed you that the sole letter I had written up to then was the one of July 12. Since my arrival in America I have received only the two communications mentioned above.

While I was away from New York, more than 20,000 Loyalists left the city for Nova Scotia, where the Crown has allotted them 500 acres of land for each family and more than 50 for each son, in addition to the amount to which Loyalists are entitled for their military service. Half pay was also given to the officers of the provincial troops organized here in America, with the exception of those who had been with the regular army and had sold their commissions to take service with the provincial troops.

The king provides ships for transporting [the Loyalists] but since there are not enough transports to accommodate the families that still remain, the evacuation of the troops from this place will not take place as soon [as expected]. Sir William [Guy] Carleton, the Commander-in-Chief, has written to the President of Congress a letter to this effect: "I have received the order to depart, but it is my duty to protect the subjects of the King I serve. Instead of implementing the recommendations made by Great Britain in the articles of peace, the United States are more loudly inveighing against the Loyalists and forcing them to leave their homeland. As a result, the number of people who request my help in obtaining transportation as well as protection during their stay in America increases daily. The evacuation of this city will take place when security will be provided for them, and the greater their number the more time will be needed."

Neither the definitive treaty nor the treaty of commerce has arrived, but some days ago it was announced that only ships owned by British subjects and of English construction could trade with the English islands. The object of this policy is to favor the commerce of Canada and Nova Scotia, and it is thought that these places will be able to supply the islands with horses and all kinds of lumber which up to now have been exported by the United States. There is certainly more moving going on here than at home. I have seen not only furniture but also entire sections of wooden houses being placed on board ship. It certainly must be very painful to leave one's homeland forever, especially to exchange it for a country which I have been told is quite disagreeable.

My being unable to write further will prove to you that I am taking advantage of the most limited opportunities to fulfill the promise which duty and gratitude prompted me to make to you. I shall leave Tuesday for Philadelphia where I shall have more time to write to you and to answer the persons from whom I have already received letters. For the present, I beg your lordship to extend my respects to Mama, relatives, and friends.

I kiss your hand with filial affection, my lord and dearest father,

Your most obliging and affectionate son,

Francesco dal Verme

[Endorsed]

Received at Voghera, November 27, 1783

3. The Southern States

October 25. Started on my journey to South Carolina. Breakfast at Chester (15 miles). Arrived at Christiana Bridge in the evening (22 miles). En route came upon the animal called *Possum*. Its general size is that of a fat, long cat with a head like a pig and a hairless tail with which it suspends itself from trees. The female has a pouch under her belly, in which (like vegetables) the young grow attached [to the mother] by the mouth; when they reach maturity they detach themselves. In case of pursuit, the mother opens this pouch, the young enter it (it closes itself), and she runs off. They are good to eat.

October 26. Arrived at *Hartford* [Bel Air ?] in the evening (40 miles). The road here begins to run in the midst of woods, and is only wide enough for a single horse. Clear.

October 27. (15 miles.) Breakfast. Passed two iron furnaces and the mine nearby.[1] Arrived at Baltimore (15 miles) by a hilly road. Dinner at the tavern. Had tea at the home of Mr. [Daniel] Dulany.[2] Spent the evening and took supper with Mr. [William ?] Hammond.[3] Clear.

October 28. Breakfast at the tavern and dinner at Mr. Hammond's. Afterwards went with Colonel [Nicholas ?] Rogers to visit the harbor, which contained many large vessels.[4] Had tea at the Colonel's house in company with various ladies among whom, next to the mistress of the house, Mrs. Taylor was the object of attention.[5] Had supper here. Baltimore, the capital of Maryland, is well built and is steadily growing.[6] Clear.

October 29. Arrived at Annapolis (30 miles). Dinner at the tavern. Went with Mr. [Daniel of St. Thomas] Jenifer to the home of Mr. [Edward] Lloyd where we had tea and spent the evening. Clear.

October 30. Breakfast at the tavern. Annapolis is the second largest town in Maryland, the seat of the Governor, and the best constructed town in America, especially the State House, but it has no commerce.[7] Congress will now meet here. When the necessary buildings are constructed, it will reside a year in Georgetown, forty miles from this place, and a year in Lamberton, twenty-seven miles from Philadelphia.[8] Dinner with Mr. Lloyd, tea with *Mrs. Stone.*[9] Cloudy and windy.

October 31. Set off with some other people (11 miles); at breakfast quarreled over the bread. Here one starts seeing the Negroes in rags and children of twelve or thirteen years almost entirely naked.[10] Took the wrong road and instead of nine miles rode 20 miles to reach Upper Marlboro, where we had dinner.[11] (In this section the taverns begin to be very bad and everything more expensive than in Philadelphia.) In the afternoon again mistook the road and went six miles out of the way (10 miles). Here I saw a fine-looking house, and since the hour was late and the wind blowing furiously and snowing, I took leave of my traveling companions (who in going twelve miles to reach the nearest inn once more missed the road) and entered the house. Mr. [George ?] Digges, the owner, received me with great courtesy and had the horses placed in the stall.[12] Had tea and supper here. His brother, a Jesuit and a man of great learning, immediately inquired whether I came from Milan; he had read in the newspaper of my arrival in America.[13] Here I also met a relative of theirs, Mr. [Thomas Sim] Lee, for whom I had a letter of introduction.[14] Windy.

November 1. Heard mass and had breakfast. In Maryland there are around twenty-five ex-Jesuits who own more than 36,000 acres of land; a square mile is 640 acres.[15] Went with Mr. Lee to the home of Captain Fitzhugh (12 miles) where we dined.[16] Crossed the Potomac River and reached Alexandria. Presented a letter to Colonel [Robert Townshend] Hooe, with whom I had dinner.[17] Clear and windy.

November 2. Left by hired horse with Colonel Hooe and with the help of a guide came to *Traincho del sela* [Trammel's Place? Turkey Island?] at the Great Fall of the Potomac River (32 miles). It is 600 feet wide and 70 high.[18] Lodged for the night (10 miles) at

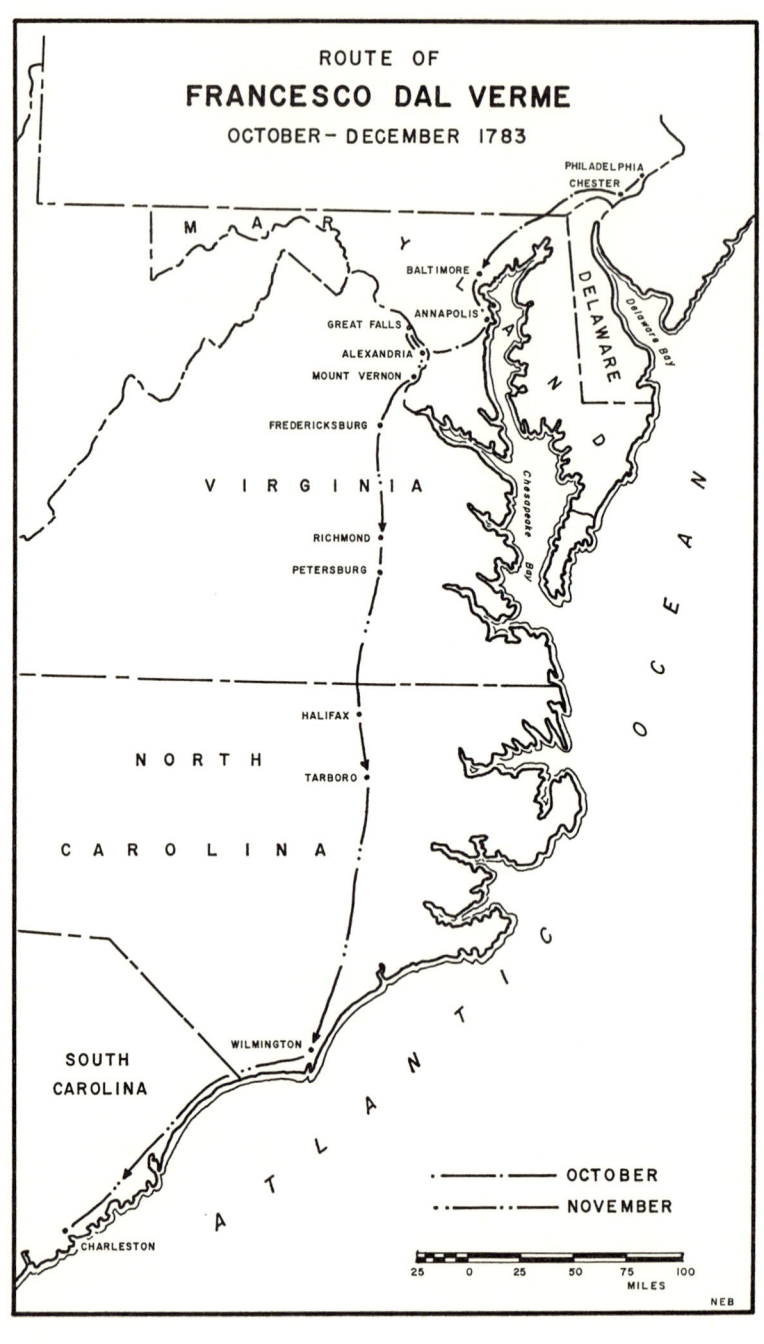

the home of a veterinarian who speaks French, German, Italian, and English. Clear.

November 3. Proceeded (12 miles) to the Little Fall of this river. Small boats come up as far as this place to take on loads of tobacco for shipment to Alexandria, which is accessible to vessels of 64 tons. Arrived at Alexandria (10 miles). Dinner with Colonel Hooe; tea and supper with Colonel Fitzhugh. Alexandria is small, but it has considerable commerce and has already grown a good deal since the peace.

November 4. Rode (10 miles) to the home of General Washington where I found only his wife and some relatives. It is situated on the Potomac River and all the vessels bound for Alexandria pass by it. The house is large. The net income of the General is estimated at 4,000 lire sterling, and the land is susceptible of much improvement. Lodged here. Clear.

November 5. Proceeded to Colchester (10 miles) and had breakfast, crossed the Occoquan Creek, and came to Dumfries (10 miles), a small place which contains two public tobacco warehouses. Dinner at the home of Colonel [William ?] Grayson; tea and supper with Mr. [John ?] Graham.[19]

November 6. (13 miles.) Breakfast. (12 miles.) Crossed the Rappahannock River, on which Fredericksburg, a small town, is situated; here there was no one for whom I had letters. Continued (5 miles) to the home of General [Alexander] Spotswood, who was away.[20] Went five miles for lodgings. Clear.

November 7. (12 miles.) Breakfast; (14 miles) refreshments; (10 miles) dinner at Hanover Court House where the court was in session. Clear.

November 8. (10 miles.) Breakfast; continued (12 miles) to Richmond, the capital of Virginia. Dined at the home of Governor [Benjamin] Harrison and spent the evening with Mr. [Edmund] Randolph. Wind, rain, and snow after dinner. Clear in the evening.

November 9. Took breakfast with Mr. [?] Smith; went to the home of Mr. [George ?] Webb (4 miles);[21] dined with Governor Harrison.

November 10. Hired a horse and rode (13 miles) to see some coal mines (26 miles). As soon as these are flooded richer ones are found on the other side of the river.²² Dinner with Mr. Randolph. Richmond, situated in a valley on the James River, is small and has very little commerce. Clear.

November 11. Crossed the broad James River. Rocks impede its navigation for ten miles above the town. A canal of six miles has been started to provide navigation for 160 miles in the interior of the country; the war interrupted this project.²³ (15 miles.) Breakfast. (10 miles.) Crossed a wooden bridge to reach Petersburg on the other side of the Appomattox River. This place is large and has considerable trade. Stayed at the home of Colonel [John] Banister (2 miles).²⁴ Clear.

November 12. Had breakfast here; (20 miles) refreshment; (7 miles) reached the home of Mr. [Henry ?] Walker.²⁵ Dinner and lodging here. Dense fog.

November 13. Breakfast with my host; (22 miles) dinner here; (9 miles) stopped for the night. In the morning was obliged to make a ditch inside and outside the door of the stall in order to lead out the horses because the doorway was too low. Clear.

November 14. (7 miles.) Breakfast; (13 miles) crossed the Roanoke River, on the other side of which is Halifax, the capital of North Carolina, a very small place with no commerce. Had dinner at the home of Mr. [Willie] Jones. Afterward went to a horse race in which small Negroes weighing around one hundred pounds served as jockeys. The purse was 12 dollars on this fourth day of racing.²⁶ The two-mile course was run in four minutes three seconds. A ball was held in the evening in a fairly large hall.²⁷ Plaques and lamps all crudely made; the supper was very good. Miss Hansen beautiful. Clear.

November 15. Dinner at the home of Colonel [Lemuel ?] Hatch, where I spent the evening.²⁸ In the afternoon went to another horse race. Clear.

November 16. (12 miles.) Breakfast; (17 miles) refreshment; (12 miles) to reach Tarboro. Clear.

November 17. (13 miles.) Breakfast; (22 miles) refreshment; (10 miles) to the home of Colonel [Jacob] Blount.[29] Clear.

November 18. Spent the day here hunting. Clear.

November 19. (22 miles.) Breakfast; (12 miles) refreshment; (8 miles) to the tavern. Clear.

November 20. (5 miles.) Refreshment; 20 miles (with no sign of a road leading to a plantation) to the tavern. Left the horses here because they had got sick from eating beans in a field. Set off on a rented horse for the home of General [John Alexander] Lillington ten miles away, but as the hour was too late for such a bad road, stopped at the home of Mr. [John ?] Williams, which I reached in the rain (6 miles).[30] In the evening after supper went fire-hunting. The hunters carry on their left shoulder a pan containing a lighted combustible for spotting the animals' eyes, which are blinded by the light and thus unable to see the hunter who approaches to within firing range of the wild beast. We came upon the trail of a panther —a fresh prey covered with leaves which had been discovered after dinner; when the panther returned to this spot, the hunter who shot it failed to kill it but only wounded it as was evident from the blood that was spattered about. One of the two deer spotted was killed. This kind of hunting is prohibited because it often results in the killing of domestic animals grazing in the woods.[31] Rain after dinner.

November 21. (6 miles.) To the home of General Lillington where my horses also came.[32] Here there was fodder, but no wine. Clear.

November 22. Breakfast. (13 miles.) Arrived at the home of Mr. [John] Swann.[33] A piece of this road is superb. Clear.

November 23. Crossed the N.E. [Cape Fear] River; the bridge over it was burned by the enemy in 1781 (13 miles). Most of Wilmington on the N.E. River was destroyed. Up to here the river is navigable to vessels of 200 tons. Dinner at the tavern. Coffee at the home of Mr. [Archibald] McLaine, where I spent the evening.[34] This town will eventually develop into a flourishing place. The tavern, kept by a Frenchman, had both fodder and wine, but the cost of everything was high in proportion to its scarcity.[35] Rain after dinner.

November 24. Crossed a bay (4 miles). Proceeded (27 miles) over an impassable road, the old one being out of use. With the aid of a guide found a lodging place. The bridges in this area, which are merely logs placed alongside each other, have all fallen down, and the traveler goes over them at some risk. The inhabitants say by way of excuse that they have not yet had time to repair them since the coming of peace. It rained while I was in the boat. Clear afterward.

November 25. Detoured a little from the road in order to reach (15 miles) the house of a person who sells food and drink but is not an innkeeper. (This [lack of accommodation] is the greatest source of irritation in the two Carolinas, where the few inns are invariably bad. The proprietors of houses which pass for ordinaries contend that they are in business solely to accommodate travelers. The price of everything is high, and the traveler dares not complain about anything, especially about the innate laziness [in providing service]. It is not unusual to have to wait one-half to one hour for a few corn shucks for the horses. After a third request for something to eat these sluggards start grinding corn for the dough which is placed over the fire to be scorched, or more correctly, to be blackened with smoke and augmented in volume with ashes. Occasionally the traveler finds a bed, but never one to himself. A room with a fireplace is the gathering place for everyone except the Negroes, whose children, however, are usually admitted; they, together with a countless number of the owner's children, make enough noise to deafen a person ten miles away. Not all places keep liquor, and very few, fresh meat.) (22 miles.) Arrived at Vareen's [?] Tavern.[36] This road is fair only because nature made it so, but the bridges are like those described above. The hind legs of my horse got caught on one of them and not until after the second try was he able to get free, and then only at great cost, as will be seen, although he reached the hostelry without giving any sign of pain. Clear.

November 26. In the morning the horse could not move his hind legs and he kept throbbing and perspiring. I exchanged him for a smaller animal in good condition. Went hunting and killed a wolf. Clear.

November 27. Rode off to hunt deer and pursued two of them without success. Downpour in the morning, clear in the afternoon.

November 28. My horse was worse and lying on the ground, but was eating. Set off at low tide (15 miles) along the seashore and found the road that turned off just by chance, since there was no kind of sign (the rule in America so far as roads are concerned).[37] (13 miles.) Came to the home of Mr. [William] Alston.[38] In the course of these twenty-eight miles there is not a single house that receives travelers. Clear.

November 29. (17 miles.) Arrived at the home of Colonel [Robert ?] Heriot.[39] South Carolina has an extensive cultivation of rice, which is consumed in great quantity and is also used in making bread. This state also produces much indigo. The [indigo] plant grows to the height of four feet and is cut three times in three months. It is then immediately placed in a wooden vat—usually twelve feet square and three deep—filled with water, and left to soak for about twenty hours. After the essence of the narrow, short leaf has been absorbed, the water is strained into another container and stirred continuously with a long spoon for twelve hours. Then a little lime water is added to settle the indigo, now reduced to a paste. The water is then drained off and the indigo transferred for drying to another vessel at the bottom of which is sand covered with a cloth. Again the indigo is removed, then put in a press to extract still more moisture, after which it is cut into tablets weighing about two ounces and placed in the sun to finish drying. An acre of good land given over to the cultivation of indigo yields a net return of 10 guineas. The plant likes rich soil and dry weather. The local price is £7.10 our money for twelve ounces. The rice grown here seems to be every bit as good as ours.[40] The potatoes are long and fat and have a chestnut flavor. They are the main source of food for the Negroes.

November 30. (3 miles.) Went by water to Georgetown. The horses crossed in a boat and I in a canoe made from a single log. It had four oars and space for six other persons besides myself. This town was almost completely burned by the enemy in 1779. Stopped here because it rained torrents all day. Rain.

December 1. (42 miles.) Crossed three rivers by boat. At Mrs. White's Tavern all the white people were away and no one had keys; consequently everything had to be obtained by breaking the doors. Clear.

December 2. (16 miles.) Came to the harbor; (3 miles) by water to reach Charleston, South Carolina, the view of which is attractive. Dinner at the tavern, tea and supper at the home of Mr. [Thomas] Ferguson.[41] Clear.

December 3. Breakfast with Mr. [Edward ?] Rutledge;[42] dinner, tea, and supper with Mr. Ferguson. Very hot wind and variable.

December 4. Breakfast with Mr. [Thomas ?] Farr.[43] Presented letters to the Governor [Benjamin Guerard], Mr. [Thomas] Bee,[44] General [William] Moultrie, Mr. [George Abbott] Hall,[45] and Mr. *Black* [William Blake ?].[46] Dinner at the home of Mr. Ferguson; at seven o'clock I accompanied him and his wife to the public ball. The hall is small because the former one was burned last year. Fifty-eight ladies were present and as many men. An elegant supper at eleven. Danced with the daughter of Dr. [Andrew] Turnbull; his wife, whom he married during his travels, is a native of Smyrna.[47] All the members of the family speak Italian well. Violent rainstorm after dinner and suffocating.

December 5. (10 miles.) Dinner; afterwards went hunting (20 miles). Clear.

December 6. Accompanied Mr. [Thomas] Farrar [?][48] (11 miles) for a dinner with the Deer Hunt Club composed of twenty-two members, who may invite friends. The hunt is held once in every fifteen days and the members take turns in defraying the cost of the repast.[49] In the evening went to the home of Mr. Farr (1 mile). Clear.

December 7. Went fire-hunting in the evening, but the moon kept us from having any success. Suffocating.

December 8. Came into town with Mr. Farr (12 miles). Dined at the *Coffee-Room* where there is a table d'hôte, and spent the evening here.[50]

December 9. Went out riding. As the town is situated on a point of land watered at the foot by the sea and on the left and right by two rivers, there is only one road that leads to it. Dinner at the home of Mr. Farr. Tea with Mr. [Ralph] Izard where I spent the evening and heard music.[51] Warm.

December 10.   Breakfast and dinner at the *Coffee-Room.* Tea and supper at the home of Mr. Bee, where we had music in the evening. Warm.

December 11.   Went to church in the morning and heard very loud music and a sermon of thanksgiving for the successful outcome of the war.[52] Subscription concert with good music in the evening; this was followed by a ball. Major [Edmund M.] Hyrne died this morning at six; he was thirty-six years old and had been wounded in the head in 1779.[53] Warm.

December 12.   Dinner at the home of Mr. Rutledge [?]. A ball in the evening at the home of the Governor to celebrate the outcome of the war; forty ladies and as many men present. Very warm.

December 13.   Rode to the home of Mr. Farr (12 miles). Using his horses, we went deer hunting with the other members of the club. Saw two deer and took one of them. It is the custom of this club to take a whole pig, split it open in the middle, place it on sticks, and roast it over embers which are placed in a hole in the ground. (They call this a *Barbachiu.*) Clear.

December 14.   Went out hunting with a gun and took many pigeons, ducks, and a hawk. After dinner returned to town (12 miles). Spent the evening at the home of Dr. Turnbull. Clear and warm.

December 15.   Breakfast and dinner at the *Coffee-Room,* where I also passed the evening. Clear.

December 16.   Dinner at the home of Mr. Izard; in the evening we had music. Mr. Izard and his wife have traveled in Italy and their daughter was educated in France. They speak a little Italian. Suffocating heat.

December 17.   Dinner with Mr. *Black* [Blake ?]. In the evening went to Mr. Farr's. A large wolf was killed in town last night by a guard.

December 18. Sent the horses to the public auction which charges a 5 per cent commission; the manager is surety for the money. Received 14 guineas for the mare and 4 for the small horse. In this town horses sell at a very low price because a large number of them have been brought here. Went on board the shallop *Hawk,* Captain *Darell* of Bermuda, to reserve passage for Antigua. Dinner at the *Coffee-Room.* A public ball and supper in the evening. Cloudy and cold.

December 19. Charleston, the capital of South Carolina, is a fairly large place, well built, but it has been greatly damaged. It contains several churches and a fine exchange whose interior, however, is almost completely ruined.[54] The main streets are regular and in parts lighted. In summer the sea breeze mitigates the noonday heat; in winter the weather is quite variable. The main streets, which are unpaved and have a sandy floor, have small walls on each side for the protection of pedestrians. The market is fairly well supplied. Charleston does not have a good public lodginghouse, and I was fortunate in finding hospitality in private homes. Nowhere, though, does one hear steady conversation and in the country the evening positively drags. There are many clubs for men who meet to gamble and smoke, both very popular pastimes. Entertainments are large, but too prevalent, and really amount to nothing. Perhaps after a year's residence one might feel at home with them.

At present America is worth a visit, traveling by land from Boston to New York and from New York to Philadelphia and by sea from Philadelphia to Charleston, where a stay of less than a month is sufficient before departure. Everything beyond this is sterile uniformity. Paid all the farewell visits. Dinner at the home of Mr. Hall. Spent the evening and had supper at Mr. Bee's, where there was music. Cold and clear.

December 20. [No entry.]

December 21. At eleven o'clock took the pilot on board the shallop *Hawk,* 120 tons, with Captain *Darrell* of Bermuda, second mate, a crew of seven men, and a cabin boy. At three o'clock, after the Captain had gone down to the fort to obtain clearance for Antigua, we reached the far end of the chain of rocks almost level with the water, called the *Bar.*[55]

The Southern States 57

Charleston, South Carolina
December 2, 1783

Dearest Father:
I don't want to fail to take advantage of the opportunity at hand to inform you at once of my safe arrival to this capital.

My journey of more than 800 miles along the road I took from Philadelphia offered little of interest. But the weather was always good—I traveled thirty-nine days without ever getting wet and stopped only two days because of bad weather—always in the best of health, and the horses never tired; all this sufficed to make a solitary and lengthy road an enjoyable and pleasant ride.

From what I have already told you thus far, you will think it strange that such a long journey does not provide enough material to fill this page. But at the very next opportunity I shall particularize at greater length down to the minutest happenings of my trip. I have not yet sent you the diary of my travels on this continent because I did not have it ready when I left Philadelphia, and since then I have had no opportunity to finish it.

My last letters to you, addressed to your lordship, Mama, Albert, and [sister] Visconti were dated October 20 from Philadelphia. I wrote three other times—July 12, August 29, and September 14. Having sent them all in care of Signor Gandolfi in London, I hope that they have arrived at their destination. The only letters I have received up to now are one from Albert and one from [sister] Visconti, both written in May. I cannot understand why others have not reached me because the arrangement for forwarding them was excellent—Gandolfi sending them to New York from where they would be sent to Charleston. I trust that I shall have news of you before long.

My plans for the last part of my journey, in accordance with the promise I had the pleasure of giving you to be in Milan by next spring, are as follows: Spend December in this city, confident that the sojourn will be entirely satisfactory. Depart from here around the first of January, 1784, for Antigua or Martinique (for which there are frequent sailings) and visit as opportunity presents itself the main ones of these little islands. From there proceed to Santo Domingo, Jamaica, and finally to Cuba, which will be the best place for obtaining passage for Marseilles. The wind regulates my tour of the islands; and according to the direction I have chosen, the wind is always from aft; consequently the passage from one island to another will be very brief.

I have obtained letters, perhaps more of them than I need, for the governors and leading inhabitants of the French, English, and Spanish islands. Up to now I have always collected for the bills of credit the same weight of gold or silver that I consigned [for them] and I believe that I shall continue to do so for the remainder of my journey.

At this season the climate is temperate but quite variable because it is entirely determined by the winds. This city, all of which I have not yet seen, appears to be large and the best constructed of any I have seen in America. Much of it, however, was burned and destroyed last year by the enemy. Even the hall for dancing suffered the same fate while the inhabitants were using it to celebrate the order received by the English to evacuate the city. What a loss! Another hall has already been substituted for temporary use, in which a ball or a concert is held on alternate Thursdays during this season.

The inhabitants have suffered very heavy property losses—the richest persons more than anyone else, since they lost their best horses, at present very high in price, countless heads of other livestock, and most of their Negroes, who cost no less than seventy and eighty guineas each if they are between the ages of twenty-five and forty. European merchandise is not very high in this city, but the products of the two Carolinas, which consist chiefly of indigo and rice, bring a good price. The former costs £7.10 per pound of twelve ounces; the latter, £24 per hundredweight.

Money is scarce and nearly all contracts are made in terms of merchandise. In the homes where I have already been introduced I have observed that the people possess every luxury enjoyed by the wealthy in Europe and that annual incomes of six, eight, and twelve thousand lire sterling are not very rare.

If at this time I am unable to write to others who should expect letters from me, I hope that they will be kind enough to put themselves in my place and forgive me. But I cannot refrain from asking you to greet them for me and to tell them that I am impatiently awaiting news of them, especially of Mama, to whom, in particular, I wish you to convey my respects. With filial respect and love, I kiss your hands and remain,

> Your most obedient and affectionate son,
>
> Francesco dal Verme

[Endorsed]

Received February 3, 1784

Charleston, December 19, 1783

Dearest Father:

I wrote to you last week, as usual, through Signor Gandolfi in London, and through the same channel I am sending this letter to which I have nothing else to add; for past news I refer you to my recent letter. Since at present there are not many sailings for the islands which I plan to see first, I am obliged to take advantage of the opportunity now available for fear that the next one might be too long off. If the wind does not change, I shall set sail tomorrow for Antigua in a shallop of 120 tons, with twelve persons on board. The average passage is of fifteen days' duration; 300 miles from this coast one encounters normal winds for the rest of the way. From that island I shall proceed after a stay of about ten days to Tobago, from where passage to all the islands is always under a favorable wind.

I am sending you the diary for these last six months, which you will immediately discover is difficult to read; but I believe that Signor Conforno [?] can prepare a copy that will be an improvement over the original, which I wrote in a hurry. You may give the latter to [sister] Visconti.

I hope that Mama will not complain if I do not write her by this post, particularly since what I am sending your lordship will suffice for both of you; and I request your lordship to reassure her of my filial respect and love.

There is nothing more to add, other than that I am with all respect,

Your most obliging and affectionate son,

Francesco dal Verme

[Endorsed]

Received at London, February 17, 1784

Received at Milan, March 13, 1784

The Southern States

Charleston, December 19, 1783

Dearest Sister:

The enclosed letter addressed to Albert and Beppo supplements, together with this journal, another one that I wish to write expressly to you. The journal is to be presented to Papa who, I suppose, will have it copied in order to read it, as it is written in minuscule. If he does have it copied, the original will be for you who are so concerned about me. These [communications] should satisfy your curiosity as to how I have spent the last six months. I don't believe the journal contains anything which might offend the eye of anyone, everything being open to a favorable interpretation. Don't expect to find anything arresting in it, which is precisely the point.

Your letter of last May mentioned something that would have distressed me had I not been certain that long before I heard of it, it would have been settled by the person able to disprove it. Enough on this subject.

What is left for me to say? I extend you a warm embrace; however, if you do not want it all for yourself, you must share with Beppo. Considering the great distance that divides us, I am certain you would not deny me this favor. Your most affectionate brother,

Francesco

4. From Charleston to Saint John's

	Miles	Latitude	Longitude	Remarks
December 21	165	31:09	78:08	
December 22	198	28:49	73:26	
December 23	148	27:26	71:07	
December 24	69	26:34	70:15	
December 25	95	25:49	68:43	Saw a ship 12 miles away
December 26	81	24:56	67:36	
December 27	101	23:54	66:08	
December 28	98	22:33	65:09	Paid for having been absent from the baptism of the tropics.
December 29	46	21:55	64:41	
December 30	88	20:53	63:35	
December 31	61	19:57	63:11	Ship 3 miles away
January 1, '84	56	19:52	62:11	Caught two four-foot dolphins
January 2	14	19:42	62:00	Spoke to a brigantine coming from Martinique
January 3	94	18:43	61:00	
January 4	100	17:32	59:45	Antigua in sight Landed
January 5	30	Antigua		

Ephrata Cloister. (Courtesy of The Historical Society of Pennsylvania)

John Bartram's house. (Courtesy of The Historical Society of Pennsylvania)

5. The West Indies

January 4. Disembarked [at St. John's] and went to the home of Mr. Smith, where I spent the evening and had supper.[1] He conducted me to an excellent lodging.[2] Fair.

January 5. Took a jaunt along the countryside where sugar production flourishes. Dinner, tea, and supper with Mr. Smith. The sun is as hot here as it is at home in July, but there is a cool breeze. Variable.

January 6. Went with Mr. *Pontew* [?] in his calash to the country seat of Governor [Thomas] Shirley (4 miles) to present the letters of introduction which I had obtained in London for him.[3] (Took breakfast here.) He speaks good Italian. Had dinner at the city tavern with the parish corporation which had that morning elected its directors. The English always terminate their public functions with a dinner at the tavern. This is always followed by a long drinking session, and sometimes the consequences are what one can expect on this sort of occasion. Had tea with Mr. *Druce* and spent the evening at the club.[4] Temperate.

January 7. Breakfast at the tavern, which is quite large and provides accommodations suitable to the climate. Dinner with Mr. [Alexander] Scott;[5] spent the rest of the day in another home. Tea and supper with Mr. Smith. Some sprinkling of rain. Warm.

January 8. Dinner at the tavern. With a hired horse rode to Parham (6 miles); returned by a different road (7 miles) which runs entirely through rich and fertile plantations and countryside. Dinner with the legislative body and the Governor (who left today to take possession of St. Christopher etc.) offered by a new member of the Assembly.[6] The Governor corresponds to the King, the Council to the House of Lords, and the Assembly, elected in the same manner as in England, to the House of Commons.[7]

January 9. Breakfast at the tavern. The western section of the town was reduced almost entirely to ashes thirty months ago. Most of the houses are made of wood and do not have a balcony to permit the continuous spraying of the roof with water in the event of fire.[8] At present, however, some houses are already covered with large sheets of an incombustible material imported from England. This seems to be a compost of chopped hemp, resin, and other [substances] covered with an oil varnish. Dinner with Mr. Smith. Tea and supper with Mr. [John ?] Burke.[9] Fair.

January 10. Dinner and tea with Mr. [John] Rose.[10] Clear.

January 11. Every Sunday the Negroes bring to the market what garden produce they do not consume.[11] Like our peasants, they are permitted to keep on their place chickens, pigs, sheep, etc. A good organ at the church.[12] Dinner, tea, and supper with Mr. Smith. Clear.

January 12. Rode to Parham with Mr. Smith to visit Mr. [Cornelius ?] Sherman with whom we had breakfast.[13] Then drove in a calash to the home of Misses [Ann and Margaret ?] Ronan on the island of Guana, which is all in pasture and yields good returns to the proprietor.[14] We were treated here to a second breakfast consisting of fish. Dinner with Mr. Sherman. Tea, game of twenty-one, and supper at the home of Misses Ronan. Clear.

January 13. Returned to my lodgings by moonlight and arrived at two in the morning (6 miles). Wrote to Papa, [sister] Visconti, and Albert. Breakfast at the tavern. Dinner with Mr. Smith. Tea and supper at the home of Misses Ronan, where we played twenty-one until three in the morning. Clear.

January 14. Dinner with Mr. Smith; tea and supper with Mr. Burke. Clear. The island of Antigua is not very large, but is extremely fertile. The countryside at present looks very promising, and the general opinion is that a little rain would increase the yield by a million sterling.[15] The present population numbers 36,000 Negroes and 3,600 whites.[16] In addition to a fixed ration of corn, salt fish, and a kind of potato called *yames,* the Negroes receive a piece of land which, with good cultivation, can supplement the lean diet provided by the master.[17] The climate renders their nakedness

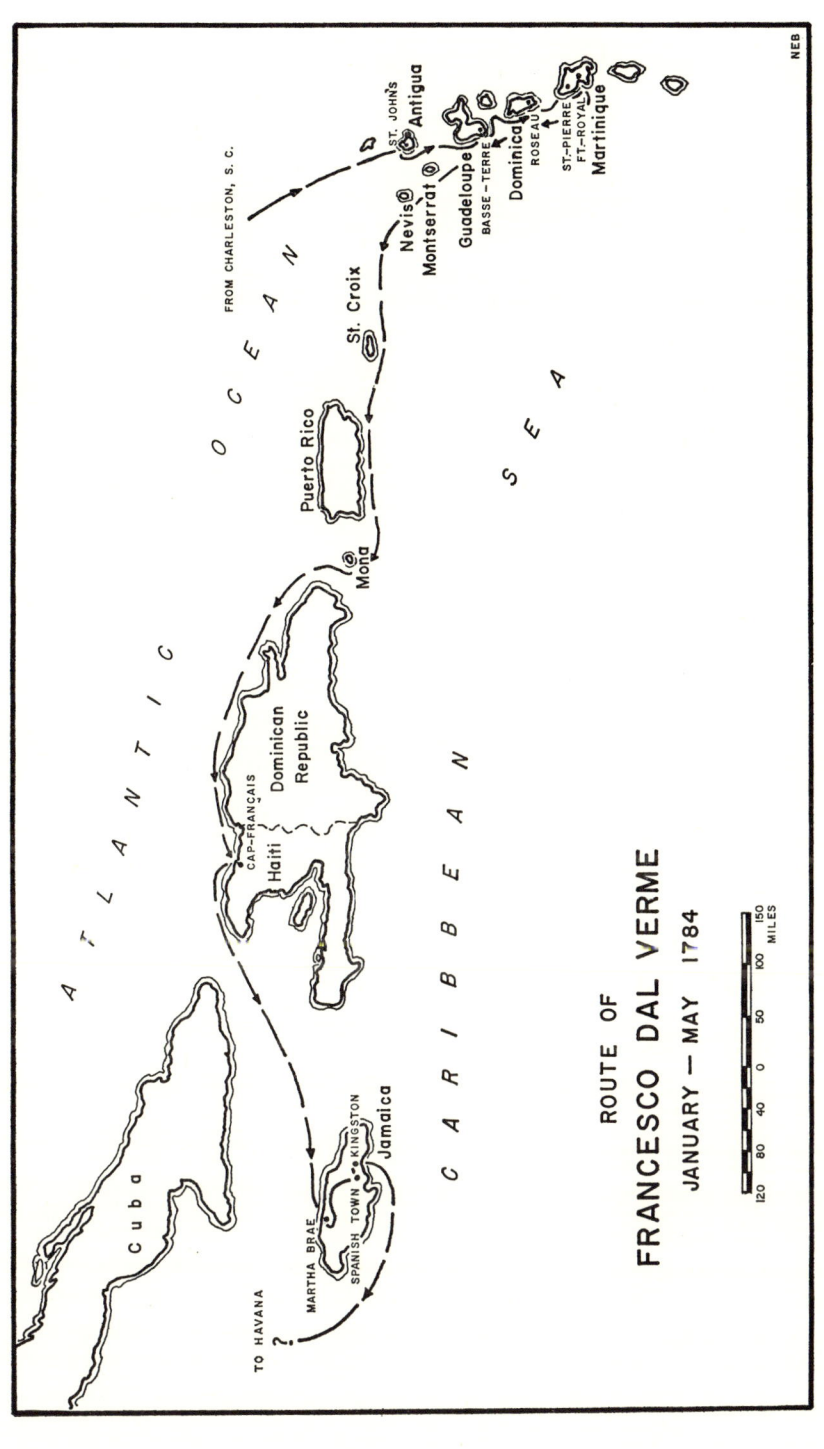

more pleasant than not. Their treatment, whether more or less cruel, depends on the disposition of those who live on the plantation.[18] St. John's, the capital, is small and modestly constructed. It was once paved, as is evident from many stones which are partly covered by mud when it rains and by dust in dry weather.[19] For six weeks now, frequent but mild earthquake tremors have been felt.[20] One night I experienced one myself. This unfailingly inspires some fear, especially among the fair sex unaccustomed to feeling something underneath them move. A troop ship arrived today from Jamaica; it took six weeks to get here, [although] the passage is considered very good. The wind is generally from the east.

January 15. Breakfast at the home of Mr. Smith. Embarked at one o'clock in a vessel of 26 tons for Guadeloupe. Sailed along the southwest coast of Antigua, which has many dangerous reefs.

January 16. Calm or contrary wind; the currents took us almost close to Antigua. Clear.

January 17. Calm. Caught a shark, much to be feared by anyone who falls into the sea. Clear.

January 18. At one at night finally came to Basse-Terre, capital of the island, only nineteen leagues distant from St. John's, Antigua. Being English, the vessel could not cast anchor; instead, the Captain accompanied by a guard had to come with me to the residence of the intendant. This official, noting that the Captain did not speak French, said that he was reluctant to impose on me in order to compensate for the Captain's avarice and ignorance and promptly directed us to the home of the interpreter. This fellow, speaking just enough English to enable him to earn eight Spanish pieces in a quarter of an hour, conducted us to the residence of the Governor, who, after inquiring about the identity of the boat and learning that it was a small vessel, merely said *"Allez, allez pour vos affaires."* [21] Mr. *Turcimanno* [Interpreter] did not derive all the profit which his compatriot had intended to afford him, for the Captain set sail on the sly leaving as compensation for all the interpreter's trouble the honor of having escorted us more than a good mile at two o'clock in the afternoon with his head uncovered—it being Sunday, he was then wearing a clean shirt and his hair was curled according to Parisian style. Went to the hotel and had dinner. After observing many troops carrying knapsacks and four field pieces, I inquired where they were going. *"Au Camp, au camp de battaille."* Quite naturally I followed them. After going a half mile the regiment arrived on a height and halted. The men then deployed in front of a small eminence on which ten gigantic soldiers nine feet high and six feet around were posted. The artillery was placed in the most advantageous location for destroying more easily the intrepid enemy and for retreating in case of *malheur*. The martial instruments, inexhaustible source of bravery in similar situations, but which certainly could not increase that of this select corps, began to fire. The colonel, displaying almost reckless courage, ran without pause from one enemy wing to another within pistol range of them. The troops, eager for a virtually assured total, but contested, victory, divided into three fire teams, each one of which fired ten shots. As soon as one squadron had finished firing it retired from the front line and the succeeding one took its place. The colonel and his aide-de-camp, who were mounted on horseback and followed by two Negro runners dressed in scarlet and gold, rode out to view the carnage which the men were inflicting on the enemy camp. If this was not completely destroyed after the first volley, it was certainly not from want of courage or mobility on the part of the commander, or of caution and art in the plan of attack, since the result earned for him honor and everlasting credit. Part of the enemy line was already stretched out cold and the remainder was barely able to stand when the artillery let loose a barrage comparable to that which took Gibraltar. As there was a garden belonging to the commander of the troops behind the position that the enemy had selected, the field pieces were only filled with powder; nevertheless they produced the same external effect of a 60 mm. piece loaded with ball and manned by a capable artilleryman. With each shot one of the unfortunate enemy was felled to the ground by a soldier hidden behind him, killed with perfect military finesse and according to the most sacrosanct rules of war. The attack completed, and reassured that not even one of this race of giants was alive, the commander placed himself at the head of his victorious troops, who were preceded by a lively band and followed by the red-hot artillery. [Together] they inspected the conquered camp, perhaps regretting the death they had inflicted on such brave opponents in the course of submission to duty. Military ardor then gave way to compassion, for not one of the enemy was deprived of either his clothes or any valuable he might have had. On the contrary [the giant silhouettes] were carried to the barracks with all the honors of war either to be preserved along with the memory of their spirited defense or to be honorably restored to the one who had contributed to their formation.[22] Clear.

January 19. Went to the Capuchin church, which is no better decorated than those near you, but is still better decorated than all the others here.[23] Spent the morning in the Council Chamber where, among other ordinances, the following one was issued: that all slaves are forbidden to ride in town because this practice has come to be regarded as very dangerous. (A gentleman who was admiring a new pair of buckles while walking had one of them crushed.) The next day I hoped to hear of the following ordinance: that whites are forbidden to ride at full speed without looking where they are going because every day this is responsible for the death of some boy, as happened to a Negro yesterday evening. But nothing of the sort occurred, perhaps because this mishap is not of sufficient importance to be reported to the judge. Two Negroes were condemned to twelve strokes of the whip for having publicly beaten a free Negro; so greatly is freedom prized by those who daily deprive many thousands of men of it, men who are no better than we are only because their status does not permit it.[24] Dinner and supper at the home of Mr. *Casamajor.* Clear.

January 20. Dinner at the tavern. Spent the evening with Mr. Casamajor. Clear.

January 21. Visited the fort, which has been made almost impregnable at an enormous cost. It is situated on an elevation and is at present almost isolated.[25] Clear.

January 22. Dinner and supper at the tavern. After dinner saw a military review. Cassava flour is a staple food here, and a Creole woman would consider it an insult to her very country if, when eating, she did not have beside her or on her knee a dish of this flour for sweetening every mouthful. I thought the flour had no flavor when eaten by itself and a disagreeable one when eaten with something else.[26] Clear.

January 23. Embarked on a schooner of 160 tons. Sailed along the eastern coast of Guadeloupe. Saw Marie Galante at five leagues

The West Indies 69

distance. At night stopped at a plantation in Dominica to take on contraband coffee.[27]

Basse-Terre, the capital of the island [Guadeloupe] is tolerably well constructed and contains a number of houses. It is situated at the foot of a chain of mountains which renders the use of calashes impracticable. Two years ago it suffered a great fire, the ravages of which are being daily repaired.[28] The houses are low in height, but of very stout construction to enable them to resist the hurricanes which strike from time to time. Clear.

January 24. Early in the morning arrived at Roseau, the capital of Dominica. Disembarked and had breakfast with a Swiss merchant. Three years ago the town was almost completely destroyed by fire and at present contains only a few houses. It will doubtless flourish if made a free port.[29] Departed at ten in the morning and at six in the afternoon arrived at Saint-Pierre, the capital of Martinique.[30] Disembarked and went to the hotel. Clear.

January 25. The church is very large, but very little frequented.[31] Went with Mr. *Parsom* to call on the Commandant. Saw a slave here whose head was exactly like that of a bat; she was called *Tamarint*. Sunday is market day for the French whites as it is for the English Negroes. The fair here is without doubt one of the best.[32] Dinner at the home of Mr. *Dyant,* who was under the impression that I had to make a sojourn on the island and insisted that I stay with him. At six o'clock went to the Comedy. The theatre is mediocre, the orchestra competent, and the troupe only fair.[33] In the evening the colored people held a dance which the whites were not permitted to watch.[34] The mulattoes, who are generally pretty, wear a headdress that resembles a sugar loaf, the top of which is covered with either a handkerchief or a veil.[35] Instead of the side-pads worn by white women, the Negroes, even wealthy ones, wear two large sacks filled with straw. Both sexes of whatever [degree of] color wear only a kind of very fine white cloak. If the forms underneath, which are not visible, appear sylphlike, imagine what such garment does to an already slender person, even though the material from which it is made might not be of the finest quality.[36] Supper at the hotel. Clear.

January 26. Left at three in the morning in a mail packet for Fort-Royal (22 miles) where we arrived at 5:30.[37] Presented the letter of the French Minister in America to the General, from whom I obtained admission to the two forts and the arsenal, which when completed will form a great square. Fort Bourbon, regarded as impregnable, is perhaps the most costly fortification of the King of France. Constructed on the summit of a hill and provided with a year's supply of water, it can accommodate 3,000 men.[38] Dinner with Mr. *Fontane* with whom I toured the harbor where ships take refuge during the hurricane season, which begins the middle of July and lasts three months. In peacetime the town is almost deserted. It is well constructed and even better paved. Departed at six in a mail cutter and arrived at Saint-Pierre at eleven. Clear.

January 27. Breakfast and dinner at the tavern. Sailed back to Fort-Royal with my baggage. Had supper and spent the night at the home of Mr. Fontane. Clear.

January 28. Visited a plantation (2 miles) and stayed for dinner. Martinique has 10,495 white inhabitants, 68,416 slaves, and 2,758 free Negroes. It has 289 sugar plantations, and 1,709 coffee, cacao, cotton, and cassava plantations; 134 mills run by water, 160 run by animals, and 13 windmills; 9,424 cattle; 1,416 sheep and hogs; 226 donkeys; 4,176 mules; and 2,604 horses.[39] Dined here and returned in the evening to the home of Mr. Fontane where I had supper. Clear.

January 29. Breakfast with the General. At ten embarked on the *Belle Alise,* 600 tons, Captain Dupuis of Messrs. George and Cottin Company, Bordeaux.[40] Had a good room. Set sail at eleven for Cap-Français. Favorable wind. Clear.

January 30. Saw Guadeloupe, Montserrat, and Nevis. Clear.

January 31. Contrary wind. Cloudy.

February 1. Sailed along the coast of St. Croix where we could see many fine plantations. Puerto Rico sighted. Clear.

February 2. Sailing close to Puerto Rico. Cloudy. Rain. In the evening headed the prow into the wind in order to lie to. Cloudy.

February 3. At the entrance of the strait between Puerto Rico and Hispaniola. Calm. Lowered a boat to heave the ship from where it

The West Indies 71

had been stranded by the current. At night lowered the anchor, which was attached to a large chain instead of a rope. Clear.

February 4. Zachee,[41] Mona, and Monica in sight. Clear.

February 5. Santo Domingo in view eight leagues away. Clear and calm.

February 6. *Vieux Cap* eight leagues away. Calm, clear.

February 7. La Grange four leagues' distance. It looks exactly like a large cow-shed with a tall haystack beside it. Calm, clear.

February 8. Cap-Français in sight. Calm, clear.

February 9. Took on board the pilot 3 miles from port, which we finally reached at two after dinner. Entrance is very difficult because of numerous reefs. Disembarked. Clear.

February 10. Changed lodgings and took one by the seaside. Presented letters to the General and others.[42] Dinner and supper at the hotel. Attended the opera and a ball.[43]

February 11. Breakfast on board the corvette *La Fansette;* dinner at the home of the General,[44] then supper, opera, and ball. Clear.

February 12. Dinner at the home of Mr. [François Jean Baptiste (?)] Gautier de la Rivière.[45] In the evening a ball at the theatre. Clear.

February 13. Dinner on board the *Fansette,* whose commander is Mr. [François Louis Joseph] de Laborde.[46] Went on board the *Amphion* to pay a visit to Mr. [Henri-Pantaléon, Comte] de Macnémara, commander of the roadstead.[47] Called on the Intendant; watched a gunnery practice in the afternoon; had supper with the General. Clear.

February 14. Dinner at the hotel—table d'hôte as usual. Opera and ball. Clear.

February 15. The church, despite its great cost, is notable only for its size.[48] This day was set aside for the celebration of peace.[49]

Dinner with all the naval officers on board the *Amphion,* a ship of fifty cannons. A table of sixty-four covers was set on deck, which was converted into a dining room by means of an overhead awning. After dinner Te Deums were sung here, and on shore at the cathedral with the General and all the municipal officers in attendance. The regular troops and militia presented arms and fired a number of volleys, as did the artillery. All the ships gave twenty-one salvos, and the merchant vessels fired without limit. In the evening there was a grand illumination in the roadstead and in the city; the one at the General's residence (formerly a Jesuit house) was very beautiful. Free opera and ball, for which tickets were distributed. The ladies were reluctant to attend because they had not been invited to supper; as a substitute an excellent buffet was set out at the end of the stage. The ball was opened by the wife of the General and her close friends. It continued with some coffeehouse keepers or women of easy manners and finished with only men, who hastened the end of the celebration by appropriating the candles for their own domestic use. There were fireworks on the stage and beautiful rockets at the home of the General, where I had dinner.

February 16. Dinner at the hotel. Rain.

February 17. Dinner at the hotel. Went to the theatre. Clear.

February 18. Went in a private carriage to the plantation of Mr. [Antoine Jean Baptiste] Walsh where I had dinner with a large group.[50] Returned to the city. Attended a ball at the theatre. Clear.

February 19. Dinner and supper at the hotel. Rain.

February 20. Dinner at the hotel. Supper at the home of Mr. [Stephen] Ceronio.[51] Rain.

February 21. Dinner at the hotel. Went to the theatre. Rain.

February 22. Dinner with the General. Went to the theatre. Clear.

February 23. Dinner at the hotel. Theatre. Supper with the General. Clear.

The West Indies

February 24. Dinner at the hotel. Theatre. Rain.

February 25. Went in Mr. *Pavoy's* carriage to his plantation, which is managed by Mr. *Avall* (6 miles). Had dinner and spent the night here.

February 26. Went on to another plantation under his management, where I had dinner. In the evening returned to Cap-Français. Supper at the home of the General. Clear.

February 27. Supper at the home of Mr. Gautier. Spent the evening with Mr. *Letout* [?]. Clear.

February 28. Dinner with Mr. *Nicolau.* Ordered the servant and baggage on board the ship *Regina Indiana.* Clear.

February 29. Embarked at daybreak on the above vessel of 250 tons bound for Jamaica. Ships leave from here only in the morning because at this time there is an offshore wind, and the pilot can conduct them out to sea. Favorable wind. Sailing along the northwest coast of the island. Clear.

March 1. Very strong wind. During the night the sea came in through the window and flooded the room, with serious damage to the contents of a trunk, which was left un-opened by its owner until a few days later. Cloudy. Cap-Français is passably large and well constructed; nearly all the houses are made of brick; the streets are regular and fairly well paved. All along the bay there is a wide quay, a mile distant from where the ships ride at anchor.[52] It is estimated that the harbor can accommodate 500 ships. The General's home is the only place that has any social activity, and it is of a monotonous sort. The place consists of a very fertile plain eighty miles by more than twenty, thirty, and forty miles in width.

March 2. Steady east wind. Clear.

March 3. Jamaica in sight. A ship spoke [to us] in the evening. Clear.

March 4. Arrived at the port of Martha Brae, in the northwestern part of the island [of Jamaica], diagonally opposite Kingston, the capital. The entry to this port is, like the place, very small.[53] Dined on board. Disembarked and had tea and supper with Captain *Mecarti*. Spent the night at the home of Mr. *Howard*. Clear.

March 5. Set off in a two-horse calash for Montego Bay (25 miles), but after eight miles one of the horses, a sorry nag, gave us to understand that it could no longer have the honor of proceeding with us. Unable to continue with only one horse, the road being steep and there being two in the carriage, we pushed on for four miles and stopped at the first plantation [we saw], the home of Mr. Winn, a Quaker (he had lived in Pennsylvania), who received us with all possible hospitality.[54] When he learned in the course of our conversation that I intended to go by land to Kingston, he interrupted to ask how I ventured to undertake a journey of one hundred miles over very high mountains with hired horses. "You shall use mine," he said, "and they certainly will not let you down in the middle of the road." After concluding that I needed four animals and a guide he said: "Day after tomorrow I shall, myself, go into town and all will be ready for your departure the following day." Such an offer was not to be scorned since it afforded the only means of making this journey with pleasure. Spent the night here.

March 6. Returned to Martha Brae. (If you have a map of Jamaica you will find on the northwest Montego Bay which is only twenty-five miles from Martha Brae.) Dinner at the tavern. Supper at the home of Captain Mecarti. Clear.

March 7. Arranged my baggage for easy transportation by muleback. Dinner, tea, and supper with Captain Mecarti. At the stated hour Mr. Winn arrived in town with everything I needed for my trip. Clear.

March 8. Emptied the trunk in preparation for shipment to Kingston by sea, with little probability, however, of its arrival there. Loaded two bundles of 35 pounds each on one mule and two beds of 20 pounds each, a tarpaulin, and a small trunk holding 33 pounds on the mule of the guide. Horse and saddle were provided for me as well as for the servant.[55] We took leave of the generous Quaker and got on our way at 10:30 in the morning. Arrived within an hour (after having crossed a river in a boat) at the home of Mr. [Edward ?] *Clark* (12 miles) where we had dinner.[56] He spent two months in Milan at the time Lord Pembroke was in that city. In proof of this he recalled an event, namely, the marriage of a very beautiful girl of the Litta family to a fat gentleman with a black beard. Continued on our way (6 miles) and slept at the home of Mr. *Fate* [William Tate ?]. The road is not very level; at the outset it runs through swampy coastland and the rest of the way through very fertile sugar plantations. Clear.

March 9. After crossing a mountain (2 miles), forded Rio Bueno, which is usually dangerous because of the many holes which cannot be seen when the water is not very low.[57] Had a man carry the baggage across on horseback; the water came up to the saddle. After traversing another high mount came to Dry Harbour (6 miles) where we had breakfast.[58] Dinner at St. Ann's Bay (15 miles) at the home of Mr. *Bidley.* Spent the night in a house owned by Mr. Winn and situated on a height. All the road is good for traveling on horseback. Clear.

March 10. Proceeded (13 miles), always over verdant hills. Only cattle and breeding horses are raised in this area. Breakfast at *Menig's* Tavern. Crossed the lofty mountain called *Mont Grand Diable* and had dinner at *Makensy's* Tavern (8 miles).[59] Spent the night at *Balling's* Tavern (6 miles). Good road. Clear.

March 11. Proceeded along the bank of the river, which winds through very high hills. Crossed the river over a bridge. Much money is being spent to make this an excellent road. Arrived (15 miles) at Spanish Town, not a very large place, but the seat of the Governor, whose residence and that of the Court of Justice, which meets four times a year, are large and fine.[60] Dinner at the home of Mr. [Hugh ?] O'Connor.[61] Came to Kingston in the evening by a difficult road (13 miles).[62] Got off at the hotel. Clear.

March 12. Breakfast at the hotel. Dinner at the home of Mr. [Richard] Lake.[63] Clear.

March 13. Dinner at the home of Mr. [Archibald] Thomson, where I spent the evening and had supper (2 miles).[64] Clear.

March 14. The church is large and has a good organ. The minister performed his duties with dispatch, and the parishioners discreetly refrained from assembling all on the same day.⁶⁵ Dinner at the home of Mrs. *Munford* (3 miles) where I spent the night. Clear.

March 15. Accompanied Mrs. Munford on a visit to Mr. [James] Pinnock, who has a very handsome house.⁶⁶ Dinner with my hostess. After dinner took an excursion in the country and the town. Had supper and spent the night in the same house as yesterday.

March 16. Returned to town in the morning (3 miles). Dinner at the hotel. Clear.

March 17. Went with Mr. Thomson to call on Admiral [James] Gambier. Dinner in town at the home of Captain [John] Porkins, the famous English privateer who captured more than 180 vessels during this war.⁶⁷ I also met here M. l'Abbé Beauregard, author of the new journal of the Antilles, who fled from Cap-Français just in the nick of time to escape arrest for having written very critically of the General of Hispaniola, Mr. Bellecombe, and others.⁶⁸ All of his possessions were confiscated. In Jamaica the patriotic scholar has found the opportunity of rendering service to his country, but, up to now, not the source of wealth which he had expected. Clear.

March 18. Dinner at the home of the Admiral (2 miles). Called on Mrs. *Thomson* and returned to town. Clear.

March 19. Dinner at the hotel. Rain in the afternoon.

March 20. [No entry.]

Kingston, Jamaica, March 20, 1784

Dearest Father:
In my letter of January 13 of this year, I mentioned having written to you from Charleston on December 19, 1783. I hope that both of these letters have arrived, as well as my journal from America sent on the same date, December 19, 1783, to [sister] Visconti. The reason for my having delayed until now to give you further news of myself is that I was waiting for a dependable occasion for sending them, like an English vessel bound for England. This is the first such opportunity. If I had chosen to write you from the French colonies (something, however, which I certainly should have hazarded) it would have meant deluding myself with the poor hope of having my letters reach you by a channel through which I do not have a settled correspondence such as I have with Signor Gandolfi in London. Today I am also writing to [sister] Visconti and sending her my journal from December 20, 1783, to the present, to be delivered to her in the same manner as the other one from America.

The state of distress I expressed in the above letters, occasioned by my having received only two letters since my arrival in America, one from Albert and the other from [sister] Visconti, dated May 10 and 12, 1783, continues and becomes daily more insupportable. If the season permitted I would repatriate before the expiration of the time you graciously allotted for my absence from home. I say if the weather permitted, because despite the fact that ships continually sail from here to Europe, beyond latitude 35° 40′ sailing becomes very disagreeable with the equinoctial winds, which usually last until the last of April.

It is pointless to give you news in this letter when you will find in the journal an account of everything that has happened. Within three or four days I shall leave for Havana; the passage usually takes a week. From there, in addition to merchant vessels which frequently sail for Europe, there is a packet that leaves every month with dispatches, but its day of departure is not fixed. In view of all this, I hope to be en route for home before or toward the middle of next April, which is precisely the nearest and most seasonable time for avoiding either heavy winds or excessive calm. I cannot know beforehand for which European port I shall find the readiest passage, but whatever it is, I am certain (given good health) it will not be many days after disembarkation that I shall have the pleasure of seeing your lordship, Mama, and others once more.

Everywhere I have been I have always had many letters of recommendation, always including some for the leading officials. For Havana I already have letters for the Governor (obtained from the General at Cap-Français to whom I had been recommended by the French Minister in America) and for six others, four of whom are among the first in birth and wealth.

I am pleased with the tour I have made of the islands, now that I have almost reached the time when I am about to see the end of it. There are too few opportunities for spending the time with either profit or pleasure: with profit, because the islands are too far removed from the centers of learning; with pleasure, because the climate and the kind of business these people engage in do not permit it. Scarcely an hour after the sun rises it burns. If one moves in the same direction as the wind he finds it suffocating; if against it, too powerful. The wind is nearly always either too mild or too strong.

People who hold land live on it. They are, for the most part, supervised by an agent, since the proprietor lives in Europe enjoying in a favorable climate the fruit of either the labor of his ancestors or that of his own early years. The merchants in the French islands work in the morning and after dinner; anyone who does not enjoy gaming finds the evenings boresome. On the English islands people come into town in the morning and remain there until two at night, then travel three, four, or five miles to return to their homes; the distance between the houses prevents frequent gatherings; consequently, there is very little society in both groups of islands; and it might be added that most of these people are not married.

I can only hope and pray that your lordship, Mama, and others have always been and are now in good health; this I am most anxious to see very soon for myself. I request your lordship to extend my respects to everyone and to share this letter with Mama just as if it were addressed to her. My health as well as that of my servant has been invariably good and I trust God may keep it so, at least until my arrival home.

Old Capitol, Richmond. (Courtesy of Virginia State Library)

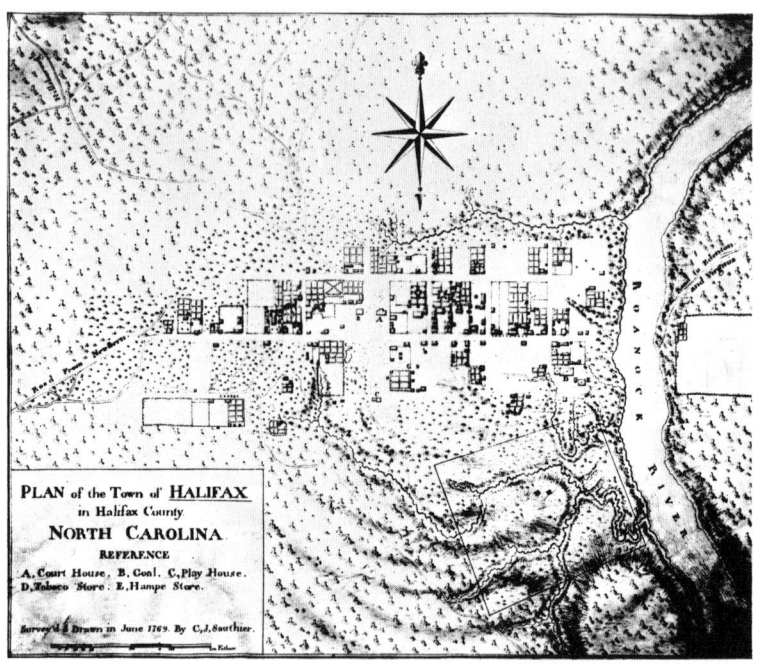

Plan of the Town of Halifax. (Courtesy of North Carolina State Department of Archives and History)

Charleston, S.C., in 1780. (Courtesy of South Caroliniana Library, University of South Carolina)

View of Basse-Terre, 1780, by Nicholas Ozanne. Engraved by Jeanne-Françoise Ozanne. (Courtesy of Archives Départementales de la Guadeloupe)

With the warmest sentiments of sincere love and filial respect, I kiss the hand of your lordship and Mama, and remain

                Your most obedient and affectionate son,

                Francesco dal Verme

[Endorsed]

Sent from London to Milan, April 30, 1784

Received at Milan, May 15, 1784

Kingston, Jamaica, March 20, 1784

Dearest Sister:

... [The first paragraph, in which he discusses mail, is omitted.]

I am enclosing in this letter my journal from the time I left Charleston, South Carolina, to today. I am sending it to you, because Papa might be out of the city, in which case it would reach you late. This way you will give it to him and request that he return it to you when he has had it copied to facilitate the reading of it. What I said concerning the nature of the other part [of the journal] applies to this one, too, namely, that the journal is written for the pleasure of the family, not of the politician.

Here I am on the last leg of my journey and this is for me a most happy prospect. At present I can conceive of nothing more pleasant than this. The distance and length of my stay from home, the lack of news since May 1783, the nature of this journey—all, all these factors contribute [to my frame of mind]. I shall not elaborate on the want of news because my spirit is not sufficiently heroic to allow me to linger over matters that are painful and irreparable. I hope that the sole and complete remedy is not far off. In three or four days I hope to leave for Havana and to arrive there before the end of this month; a sojourn of twelve or fifteen days will bring us to the middle of April, a perfect time for undertaking with less inconvenience and more pleasure a voyage of four or five weeks. Barring a mishap, on disembarking I am taking whatever means are available by land for traveling home with speed and pleasure. According to this plan, which is not beyond realization, I am almost certain of being at home before the end of spring, as I have written to Papa in explanation of the insurmountable obstacles facing an earlier arrival and what it means to travel in winter in order to arrive at the beginning of spring. Yet the difference [in time] is so inconsequential that it has only a metaphysical significance. What you can take on my word of honor is that I have always availed myself of the first opportunity to pass from one island to another.

The West Indies

Not one of the island cities requires a lengthy stay in order to profit from the cultural advantages and diversions it provides. Indeed, there is so little society that it is almost difficult to determine whether or not it exists. The climate is too different from the type that agrees with me; to be obliged to remain indoors for most of the day, without experiencing the pleasure of a jaunt in the country, is certainly not the most effective way of diminishing the longing for friends. But having always enjoyed perfect health, never having suffered any mishap, having been recommended everywhere and introduced into the best homes, having had sufficient inner strength to sustain every event with decorum without relying on ruinous sources of relief—this chain of happy circumstances at least renders my situation less unpleasant than you might imagine. If such happy auspices continue to prevail until my return to the homeland of him who first visited this continent, oh with what pleasure we shall dwell on all of this.

In this letter I have already referred to the lack of news since May 12, 1783. I am now suggesting the speediest way for you to enable me to have news of the family, which might be of interest to me, from the above date to the day you receive this letter. The two ports of Spain, at one of which it seems most certain I shall arrive, are Cadiz and Corunna. Through Count Greppi you can send two identical letters containing the news I seek to the House of Greppi in Cadiz; one [is] to remain there, the other one [is] to be sent by the recipient to the postal office at Corunna with specific instructions to hold it until the person to whom the letter is addressed picks it up. If I arrive at Cadiz I go to the House of Greppi and find your letter; if I arrive at Corunna I go to the post and get the other one. I have every reason to hope that you will comply with my reasonable request, although there is little probability that this letter will reach London and eventually Milan, and that your letters reach the above ports before I arrive at one of them. Yet this [plan] might materialize, in which case it will be one of the happiest occurrences that could befall me on my return.

If you have received the letter that I wrote you from Falmouth on May 14, 1783, you will have found enclosed a paper containing [a statement of] the sum of money that I had remaining on that day after paying for the passage to America. My travels on the continent as well as on the islands cost me from one day to another one of the units of currency [lire sterling] in which I computed the above statement. Add to it about 70[lire] to pay for my passage from

Havana to Europe and you will see how much I still have for traveling home, namely, more than I need.

What more can I say, other than that you greet everyone for me, that I embrace you, and that I am,

Your most affectionate brother,

Francesco

I am not writing to Beppo because you are often together and you know that so far as I am concerned Beppo, you, and Albert are as one.

Havana, April 12, 1784

Dearest Father:
March 21 [20] was the date of the letter I sent you from Jamaica by way of London, and since this is a dependable channel I have not the slightest doubt that the letter has already arrived, along with the one containing my journal of the islands sent to [sister] Visconti, which she will have delivered to you.

My voyage from Jamaica to this city was excellent, but longer than it ordinarily takes, since we embarked on the 25th of last month and arrived here on the night of the 8th of this month. This letter will go by packet to Corunna; from there Signor Barela, a rich merchant of this place to whom I have been recommended, will arrange to have it sent to his brother in Cadiz, and from there to Signor Belloni in Genoa, who will forward it to you in Milan.

According to the information that I have been able to obtain in these three days, I am confident that I shall leave for Europe this month, for which port I do not yet know, but I am almost certain it will be for either an English or a French, rather than a Spanish port, since the northern ports of Spain have no ready means for proceeding home, and the southern ones are menaced, although remotely, by corsairs.

This city, with which I am still unacquainted because of its size, is, undoubtedly, from that standpoint as well as from its architectural features and other factors, the leading one in these islands. So far I have had only the opportunity to witness religious ceremonies, which have been very numerous and full of pomp. Last night saw the opening of the theatre which, in contrast to the bad company, appears all the more handsome and large. On holidays after dinner everyone is transported outside the city by means of a chair drawn by a single mule ridden by a Negro. There is an infinite number of these vehicles which one rents by the hour. Even the shoemaker would consider it demeaning not to possess one of these conveyances for being carried through the city, whose streets, although small, are not made for walking, being uneven, unpaved, very dusty when dry, and even more muddy when wet.

I would not have the time, [even] if I had the material, to prolong this letter. What I shall learn about this place in the course of my sojourn here, I hope to tell you in person before long.

Our health is excellent, and I hope that the same goes for yours and Mama's, whose hand and that of your lordship I kiss with filial respect. Please convey my regards to everyone. I am,

Your most obedient and affectionate son,

Francesco dal Verne

The West Indies

Havana, April 13, 1784

Dearest Sister:
Tomorrow the packet leaves for Corunna and, via Cadiz, for Genoa. I hope this letter will reach you about the first of next month. You may wonder why the mailboat is leaving and I am not. According to what I wrote you in my last letter (March 21) from Jamaica, I should have arrived here fifteen days ago. This was my hope, but it has not been realized.

I left Jamaica on the 25th of last month and did not arrive here until the night of the 8th of this month. There are frequent sailings here for Cadiz, and once a month a packet leaves for Corunna, but from the information I have obtained thus far, I have reason for hoping to find passage this month either for England, on an English vessel, or for some French port in the Bay of Biscay, on a French vessel. Whichever it may be, I am disembarking wherever it will be easy to reach home. Such is not the case at Spanish ports, in the southern ones of which there is some danger, although remote, from pirates. Oh you see with what precaution I am regulating my departure! And I hope to be in winter quarters fifteen days after the arrival of this letter; should this not happen, you must not be alarmed about me, since calculations for a sea voyage are problematical.

In my letter of the 21st of last month, I had asked you to send me news of home from May 1783, the date of the last letters I received from you, at Corunna and Cadiz. Now that I feel almost certain that I shall not be going to either of these places, I should be very pleased to receive such news at Turin, *chez* Signor Morelli, Court Banker, by whose house I shall undoubtedly pass.

A five-day stay in a Spanish city during the last two days of Holy Week and the Easter holidays is just enough to learn only the streets and the exterior of the very many houses (these are built without plan from a stone which is the common foundation of the city and its environs; it looks like soap when it is excavated and hardens when exposed to the air). Although the straight, unpaved streets are very narrow, they form a large city enclosed by a wall like that of Genoa. There are many churches well built and richly ornamented and many churchmen, proportionately ten times more than at home. Widely used are gigs driven by a single mule, cloth mantles, *oglia,* and Dons. The American and Italian houses to which I was recommended are of great service to me. I have dined with the Intendant and the Commander of the Navy, both of whom hold themselves very much aloof from the people. The Governor has received my letter. No one wants to stay at home, but must show himself at the *corso,* each in his own carriage.

The Americans, who may ship only lumber to the French islands and are probably engaged in illicit trade with the English, are totally excluded from the Spanish islands, as are all other nations. Moreover, within a month the Americans must leave the Spanish dominions. It is believed that America will close its ports to all vessels sailing from these and other Spanish ports which exclude American shipping. If war in Europe, which everyone here expects, does not occur, American commerce will suffer very much.

My health is good and I trust that yours is the same. I am not mentioning some persons; Beppo and Albert I pass over in silence. All my respects to the others,

Your brother,

Francesco

Appendixes

Appendix I

Expences (in which those of Governor Clinton and other gentlemen who accompanied me are includid) on a Tour to crown point to the northward—and Fort Schuyler and Otsego lake to the westward.[1]

1783 July			
at Kender Hook		16	
Cohoos and the Ferry near them	2	17	6
widow-Javer	11	4	
Ferryes near Saratoga going and returning	2	4	0
Tavern at Fort Edward	10	6	8
Fort George going and returning	4	0	0
carring place between Lake George and Lake Champlain transporting Boats and other charges	7	9	4
Crown point	1	12	0
Putnams-Do		16	
Ticonderoga		16	
Fort Edward-returning	9	10	
Balls Town	1	4	
Tavern 5 miles from Schenectady	8	6	
Ditto at old Fort Johnson	6	12	
Ditto-sundries at and near Fort Rensalear	4	10	
German Flats	3	6	
Paid the Batteau men at Schenectady	2	8	
Whashing-and servants at diffet places	3	4	
To Major Glens account for Horse hire &c pr mn	38	2	
carried over +	124	13	6
	119	3	6
Over added [in different handwriting]	5	10	

1. Washington Papers, Series 5, XXIV, 89, Lib. Cong.

		Brought over	124	13	6
Aug. 3		To cash advanced the assist^t quarter master to enable him to procure Boats and to defray other Expences of the journey in his line viz 50 Dollars a 8/	20		
			£144	13	6
		Deduct 33⅓ differ^s of Exchange between york curr^y & lawful money	36	3	4
		Lawfull money	£108	10	2

Appendix II

Yale College, Sept. 10, 1784

Sir

You may be pleased herewith to receive, through the hands of M. Letombe the Consul General of France at Boston, the Diploma of an honorary Degree of *Doctor in Laws,* by the unanimous Vote of our Senators Academiens, conferred upon you, at our public anniversary commencement last year—We ask your Acceptance of this Testimonial of our respect to a learned foreign Nobleman; whose ardent Love of Liberty, whose juvenile acquisitions in Literature, whose Thirst for Knowledge and an augmentation of his Treasure of Wisdom, by conversing with the Literati of all Nations, and by an extensive acquaintance in Travels with Life & Manners, Law & Politics, presage & ensure one of the future shining Characters, both in the literary & political World—I am happy to have had the Honour of conferring this Degree upon a Personage of your Eminence for Patriotism, and extensive Benevolence to Mankind, and generous Love of every Thing—which tends to enlarge & enoble the human Mind; aggrandize the Republic of Letters, purify, improve meliorate & perfect the political systems of national Policies & Governments, so as to rescue Mankind into *Liberty* & *Happiness.* May your liberal & exalted Ideas, impregnate the Princes & Nobility of all Nations, & diffuse themselves thro' every Kingdom, Empire & Republic on Earth until human Nature shall be advanced to the highest Perfection, it is susceptible of on this side Imortality.

I inclose also an inaugural oration with a catalogue of this university.[1] Your Name will be printed in future catalogues, tho' inadvertantly omitted in this. I send you also the History of Yale College, by the late president Clap. I have the Honour to be &c.

Ezra Stiles

To the Count Francescus Dal Verme LL.D.
a Nobleman of Milan in Italy.

> Sept. 11, 1784. Sent with the Diploma to M. Letombe by Messrs. Tutors Russell & Baldwin.

1. The Inaugural Oration and Catalogue, as well as a translation of Stiles's letter, are in the Dal Verme Archives.

Appendix III

Boston, June 1, 1785

Dearest and most esteemed friend:

The desire to give you news of your friends in America and the opportunity of sending you the diploma of Doctor in Laws from the University of New Haven [Yale] afford me the favorable excuse for entering into correspondence with you.

Mr. Letombe, the French consul, from whom I received the annexed packet, and Messrs. Breck, Bowdoin, Swan, Knox, etc., as well as various ladies, among them Miss Temple, Miss Sheafe, and other pretty unmarried American nymphs, remember you quite vividly; they have eagerly asked for news of you, and request me to extend their greetings to you.

I take this opportunity to present my respects to your sister, Marquise Visconti, to Count Costanzo, and to Beppo Taverna, at the same time hoping to be counted among your servants and friends. With the highest personal esteem,

I am,
Luigi Castiglioni

Appendix III

Philadelphia, December 6, 1785

Dearest Friend:

In the course of my journey in these parts of America, I learned that you had lost a box containing some of your things and even some of your writing; since I am not wanting in diligence when it comes to serving my friends I had the good fortune to find it at Philadelphia, in the hands of Sigr. Gouverneur Morris who, not knowing to whom he should send it, had long forgotten about it.

This will come to Milan countersigned with the letters A^{c}C Number 2, together with a case of seed directed to my brother. Fearing that after so long a time the contents of the box would have been damaged by dampness, I thought it wise to open it and found the valise completely dry and in good condition. You will find in the straw a green wax candle and a few seeds which I request you to save for my brother.

I extend regards from all your friends here, and hoping that I may be counted among them, I am most sincerely,

Your affectionate and obliging friend,

Luigi Castiglioni

Notes

Notes to Introduction

1. New York *Royal Gazette,* July 2, 1783.
2. Jane Carson, *Travelers in Tidewater Virginia* (Williamsburg, Va., 1965), xi–xx; Lester J. Cappon, "The South during Two Wars," in *Travels in the Old South,* ed. Thomas D. Clark (Norman, Okla., 1956–59), I, 149–307; William B. Hamilton, "The Post Revolutionary War South, 1783–1865," *ibid.,* II, 73–165.
3. John Adams' *Diary* contains the following entry under Apr. 28, 1783: "Mr. Hartley [David Hartley, British Peace Commissioner] desired of me Letters of Introduction for Il Comte di Fermé a Cousin of the Neapolitan Ambassader in London, who is going to America, which I promised him and wrote in the Evening." The letters of introduction were addressed to John Hancock, James Bowdoin, and Benjamin Lincoln (John Adams, *Diary and Autobiography,* ed. L. H. Butterfield [Cambridge, Mass., 1961], III, 113 and n.).
4. Henry Grand to William T. Franklin, n.d., Letters to William Temple Franklin, VII, 77, Franklin Papers, American Philosophical Society Library. Ferdinand Grand was Paris banker of the U.S. Treasury. John Adams wrote a gossipy little sketch of Ferdinand Grand and his family connections (Adams, *Diary,* IV, 64–65; II, 303n.; I. Minis Hays, ed., *Calendar of the Papers of Banjamin Franklin in the Library of the American Philosophical Society* [Philadelphia, 1908], IV, 114, 338).
5. Teresa dal Verme married Prince Caramanico in 1725. Lodovico Belgioioso (1728–1801), Knight of Malta, participated in the Seven Years War and was minister plenipotentiary at Stockholm in 1765. Graf Friederich Kageneck served in London from 1783 to 1786 (Pompeo Litta, *Famiglie Celebri Italiane,* Fascicolo 30, Tavola III; *London Calendar for the Year 1783* [London, 1783], 92).
6. Franklin to Robert R. Livingston, Apr. 27, 1783, *The Works of Benjamin Franklin,* ed. John Bigelow (New York, 1904), X, 110–11.
7. Charles K. Bolton, *Bolton's American Armory* (Boston, 1964). Washington had the family crest placed on plates, harness, carriage, cane, stone seal, fireplace plates, bookplates, and other objects.
8. Litta, *Famiglie Celebri,* Fascicolo 30, Tavola I; *Annuario della Nobiltá Italiana,* XVIII (1896), 1193–94, 1197.
9. The principal sources of information on the Dal Verme family have been: Litta, *Famiglie Celebri,* Fascicolo 30, Tavole I–III; "Dal Verme," *Famiglie Nobili in Lombardia* (Milan, n.d.), Tavole I, II; Luigi Bignami, *Sotto l'Insegna del Biscione—Condottieri Viscontei e Sforzeschi* (Milan, 1934), 41–85; M. Tabarrini, *Francesco Petrarca e Luchino Dal Verme* (Rome, 1892); Giuseppe Mazza, *Il Conte Luigi Dal Verme Signore di Voghera e di Bobbio Dalla Condotta Veneta a quella Viscontea 1424–1436* (Casteggio, 1964); *Annuario della Nobiltá Italiana,* XVIII

(1896), 1193–98; Giuseppe Gerola, "Luoghi e Persone di alcune Lettere del Petrarca," *Nuova Antologia* (July, 1908), 3–7; *Storia di Milano* (Milan, 1953–62), *passim;* Ernest E. Wilkins, *Petrarch's Eight Years in Milan* (Cambridge, 1958), 104–5, 246–47.

10. Quoted in Bignami, *Sotto l'Insegna del Biscione,* 47.

11. Franco Valsecchi, "Dalla pace di Aquisgrana alla battaglia di Lodi," *Storia di Milano,* XII, 314–16; Giovanni Seregni, "La Cultura Milanese nel Settecento," *ibid.,* XII, 624.

12. Count Karl Joseph Firmian (1718–82) (*Enciclopedia Italiana,* XV, 463–64; Ottavio Barié, "La Cultura Politica dell' Età delle Riforme, *Storia di Milano,* XII, 419–57).

13. The editor is greatly indebted to Count Gian Carlo dal Verme for this and other information concerning his family.

14. Litta, *Famiglie Celebri,* Fascicolo 30, Tavole III.

15. Ettore Rota, "Milano Napoleonica," *Storia di Milano,* XIII, 12 ff.; Mme Jeanne [Jehan d'Ivray] Fahmy-Bey, *La Lombardie au Temps de Bonaparte* (Paris, 1919), 64, 75, 252–53; Francesco Melzi d'Eril, *Memorie—documenti e lettere inedite* (Milan, 1865).

16. D'Eril, *Memorie,* I, 373–76, 555, 569; II, 561; *Storia di Milano,* XIII, 84, 229.

17. In 1826 Count dal Verme refused the office of podesta (G. B. Marchesi, "Il Podestà di Milano Conte Antonio Durini," *Archivio Storico Lombardo,* 3rd ser., XX [1903], 172).

18. Guglielmo Barblan, "L'Ottocento e gli Inizi del Secolo XX," *Storia di Milano,* XVI, 700; Irving Kolodin, "The Genesis of the Inexplicable," *Saturday Review,* Mar. 25, 1967, pp. 62–63.

19. Washington to William Fitzhugh, Sept. 24, 1783, Washington Papers, CCXXV, 65, Lib. Cong. At this time Washington also wrote letters in behalf of Dal Verme to Govs. William Paca, Benjamin Harrison, and Thomas Nelson and to Archibald Cary and John Fitzgerald (*ibid.,* CCXXV, 67). Similar letters had been written on Aug. 4, 1783, to Govs. Jonathan Trumbull, William Greene, and Meshech Weare, Gen. John Sullivan, John Langdon, Nathaniel Tracy (*ibid.,* CCXXIII, 122; Weare's letter is in the Dal Verme Archives, Milan).

20. See Appendix I, "Expences . . . on a Tour to crown point to the northward," above, pp. 89–90; Washington to Daniel Parker, Sept. 18, 1783, *Writings of George Washington,* ed. John C. Fitzpatrick (Washington, D.C., 1931–44), XXVII, 154–55.

21. Luigi Castiglioni (1757–1832) was the son of Count Ottavio Castiglioni and his wife, Teresa, daughter of the renowned Count Gabriele Verri. Among Luigi Castiglioni's many honors were memberships in the American Philosophical Society and the Società Patriottica of Milan. In Lombardy he served for varying periods as director of the royal printing office and president of the Academy of Fine Arts. He was a senator of the Kingdom of Italy, Knight of the Iron Crown, and Chamberlain of the Emperor of Austria. His reputation in Europe rests largely on his having introduced there the robinia, catalpa, yellow poplar, and other native American trees and on his having assembled a valuable coin collection which is now in the Castello Sforzesco (Nicola Cané, "Luigi Castiglioni uno che

Introduction 99

conobbe l'America del Nord un secolo e mezzo fà," *L'Ambrosiano*, No. 226 [Sept. 22, 1941], 3). One of the reviewers of Castiglioni's book, *Viaggio Negli Stati Uniti dell'America Settentrionale fatto negli anni 1785, 1786, 1787* (2 vols., Milan, 1790), observed that Castiglioni's travels were both purposeful and fruitful, since a large number of the plants he had brought from America were flourishing on the Castiglioni estate near Milan (*Opuscoli Scelti sulle Scienze e sulle Arti*, XIII [Milan, 1790], 17–18). Castiglioni's herbarium and a large painting showing him holding his two volumes of *Viaggio*, which unfortunately was badly damaged during World War II, are in the villa of Marchese Cornaggia Medici at Mozzate (Gabriele Cornaggia Medici, *Cenni Storici sulla Cappellania di S. Bartolomeo di Mozzate* [Milan, 1926]; other information provided through the courtesy of Marchesa Elisa Cornaggia Medici). Authorship of *Storia delle Piante forastiere le più importanti nell'Uso Medico, od Economico colle loro Figure in Rame Incise Da Benedetto Bordiga* (4 vols., Milan, 1791) has been attributed to Castiglioni. This work contains very fine engravings.

22. "Memorandums taken on a journey from Paris into the Southern parts of France, and Northern of Italy, in the year 1787," *The Papers of Thomas Jefferson*, ed. Julian P. Boyd (Princeton, N.J., 1950–), XI, 436–40.

23. Helen Duprey Bullock, *My Head and My Heart* (New York, 1945), 181–86.

24. Jefferson to Dal Verme, Aug. 15, 1787, Dal Verme Archives. Jefferson probably sent to Dal Verme a copy of the Stockdale edition of the *Notes on Virginia*, which was ready for public distribution in July 1787 (Thomas Jefferson, *Notes on the State of Virginia*, ed. William Peden [Chapel Hill, N.C., 1955], xvi–xx). The other works were David Ramsay, *History of the Revolution of South-Carolina* (2 vols., Trenton, 1785), or *Histoire de la révolution d'Amérique, par rapport à la Caroline Méridionale* (2 vols., London, 1787); and François Soulès, *Histoire des troubles de l'Amérique anglaise* (2 vols., London, 1785), or a four-volume edition of this work which was published in Paris in 1787.

25. Jefferson to Dal Verme, July 13, 1788, Dal Verme Archives; see also Elizabeth Cometti, ed., "Mr. Jefferson Prepares an Itinerary," *Journal of Southern History*, XII (Feb. 1946), 89–106; Cometti, "John Rutledge, Jr., Federalist," *ibid.*, XIII (May 1947), 186–219. A letter from George Abbott Hall of Charleston, S.C. (May 12, 1785), introducing James and Nathaniel Heyward is in the Dal Verme Archives.

26. In his letter of thanks to Dal Verme, Oct. 22, 1788, Shippen added this postscript: "Have the goodness to lay me at the feet of the fair ladies to whom you were so kind as to present me, and to say to them how much I was charmed with their acquaintance—Say to Count Taverna that I never advanced so rapidly in the acquaintance of any one nor ever formed a more sudden attachment than I have for him." Rutledge wrote in a similar vein, Apr. 28, 1789: "I retain the most grateful sense of the kindness with which you honored me whilst at Milan, shall, thro' the whole course of my life, look back with pleasure, to that part of it, I passed there." Rutledge's postscript also paid tribute to the ladies: "Pray make my friendly compliments acceptable to that paragone of earthly excellence the Countess de

Litta & also the charming & amiable Mad^{me} de Castiglione" (both letters are in the Dal Verme Archives). Countess Litta and Rutledge had a brief exchange of letters (see Rutledge letters and Diary, Rutledge Papers, Duke University Library; Diary and Journal of Thomas Lee Shippen, 1788, Shippen Papers, Lib. Cong.).

27. Shippen exaggerated about the capacity of the boxes at La Scala, which can accommodate no more than nine persons (Thomas Lee Shippen to William Shippen, Oct. 20, 1788, Shippen Papers, III, No. 33, Lib. Cong.).

28. This promemoria and the letters and journal used in the preparation of this resumé of Dal Verme's travels are in the Papers of Count Francesco dal Verme, Dal Verme Archives.

29. Rear Admiral Richard Kempenfelt, commander of the *Royal George*, was in his cabin when the disaster occurred, Aug. 29, 1782; he went down with the ship (*DNB*).

30. Probably Major General Augustine Prevost (d. 1786). The account of Dal Verme's travels in Scotland is contained in a letter to Margherita Visconti written in Glasgow, Oct. 11, 1782, and one to his father, written in Edinburgh, Sept. 27, 1782.

31. Henry, third Duke of Buccleuch and fifth Duke of Queensberry (1746–1812); William John, fifth Marquess of Lothian (1737–1815); James, third Earl of Hopetoun (1741–1817); Douglas, eighth Duke of Hamilton (1756–99). *Daniel in the Lions' Den*, formerly in the collection of the Duke of Hamilton, Hamilton Palace, was sold at Christie's, Nov. 6–7, 1919. A study for the painting is in the J. Pierpont Morgan Library, New York (Julius S. Held, *Rubens Selected Drawings* [London, 1959], I, 131–32).

32. The account of Dal Verme's travels in Ireland is contained in a letter to his sister from London, Dec. 10, 1782, and two to his father— from Dublin, Oct. 17, 1782, and from London, Nov. 29, 1782.

33. Robert Jocelyn, first Earl of Roden (1721–97), was appointed auditor general of Ireland in 1750.

34. General John Burgoyne was made commander-in-chief in Ireland on June 7, 1782.

35. To Count Antonio dal Verme, London, Mar. 25, 1783.

36. See enclosure in letter to Margherita Visconti, Falmouth, May 14, 1783 (p. 4).

37. Count Antonio's epistolary record shows that he replied promptly to his son's letters from America, all but one (Jan. 13, 1784) of which he received. The westbound letters were sent to London in care of Gandolfi who was to forward them to America.

38. Draft of a letter to a friend in America, n.d.

39. To Count Antonio dal Verme, July 7, 1784. Like Dal Verme, Castiglioni paused in England to acquire proficiency in the English language (Howard R. Marraro, "Count Luigi Castiglioni," *Va. Mag. of Hist. and Biog.*, LVIII [Oct. 1950], 473–91).

40. *Travels in the Confederation* [1783–1784] *from the German of Johann David Schoepf*, tr. and ed. Alfred J. Morrison (Philadelphia, 1911; 1st ed. in German, Erlangen, 1788), I, 3.

Introduction

41. The authors of the following travel accounts published after 1788 were in the United States in 1783 and/or 1784: *Our Revolutionary Forefathers: The Letters of François Marquis de Barbé-Marbois . . . 1779–1785,* tr. and ed. Eugene Parker Chase (New York, 1929); George Hanger, *The Life, Adventures, and Opinions of Col. George Hanger,* ed. William Combe (2 vols., London, 1801); Johann Conrad Döhla, *Tagebuch eines Bayreuther soldaten, des Johann Conrad Döhla aus dem nordamerikanischen freiheitskrieg von 1777 bis 1783* (Bayreuth, 1913); Francisco de Miranda, *The New Democracy in America: Travels of Francisco de Miranda in the United States, 1783–84,* tr. Judson P. Wood, ed. John S. Ezell (Norman, Okla., 1963; 1st ed. in Spanish, New York, 1928).

42. Letter of Dec. 19, 1783 (see p. 61).

43. To Margherita Visconti, Dec. 10, 1782, and undated draft of letter to Messrs. Hall, Parsons, Ceronio, Seagrove, Webb, Dal Verme Archives.

44. Miranda, *Travels,* 69. See also Seymour Dunbar, *A History of Travel in America* (Indianapolis, 1915), I; Elise Lathrop, *Early American Inns and Taverns* (New York, 1926); Alice Morse Earle, *Stage-Coach and Tavern Days* (New York, 1922). For some of the roads covered by Dal Verme, see Christopher Colles, *A Survey of the Roads of the United States of America, 1789,* ed. Walter W. Ristow (Cambridge, Mass., 1961).

45. Castiglioni reported, however, that the road from Georgetown to Charleston was, with the exception of the one from Boston to Portsmouth, the finest in the United States (*Viaggio,* I, 233; see also Robert Hunter, Jr., *Quebec to Carolina in 1785–1786,* ed. Louis B. Wright and Marion Tinling [San Marino, Calif., 1943], 282–86).

46. Hunter called Niagara Falls "perhaps the greatest natural curiosity in the world, certainly the first of its kind and which people come from all parts of the world to see" (*Quebec to Carolina,* 99–100). Some years later (1825) Count Carlo Vidua wrote that Niagara Falls was the one sight that had lived up to his great expectations of it (*Lettere del Conte Carlo Vidua* [3 vols., Turin, 1834], III, 142–44).

47. Jefferson, *Notes,* ed. Peden, 19–20, 24–25.

48. See Marquis de Chastellux, *Travels in North America in the Years 1780, 1781 and 1782,* ed. Howard C. Rice, Jr. (2 vols., Chapel Hill, N.C., 1963), I, 104–5, 200–201; Constantin F. C. Volney, *Tableau du climat et du sol des États-Unis d'Amérique* (2 vols., Paris, 1803), 125–26; Castiglioni, *Viaggio,* I, 163–64; Miranda, *Travels,* 94; Médéric Louis Moreau de Saint-Méry, *Moreau de St. Méry's American Journey,* tr. and ed. Kenneth Roberts and Anna M. Roberts (New York, 1947), 116.

49. John Ferdinand D. Smyth, *A Tour in the United States of America* (2 vols., London, 1784), 90–103; Abbé [Claude C.] Robin, *Nouveau voyage dans l'Amérique Septentrionale, en l'annee 1781* (Paris, 1782), 146–47; Castiglioni, *Viaggio,* II, 47–48.

50. *Viaggio,* I, 367–68.

51. These were typical comments: "Game is very plenty here, particularly deer, beavers, otters, raccoons, and that very extraordinary animal, the opossum, the female of which has a double, or false belly: within it the young ones grow to the teats, like fruit to the stalk, and drop off at a

certain period. After she has brought forth her young, during the season of their infancy, whenever they perceive the danger nigh, they all run into the mother's bag, or false belly, for security and refuge" (Smyth, *Tour of the United States*, I, 93).

"The rattlesnakes first come forth from their dens into the sunshine of the early spring, sun themselves the whole day long and then in the evening they crawl back again. . . . Colonel Lydius once found a great number of them in one place and he shot sixteen of them. His companion beat several to death, and the rest of them lay under a large stone and rattled vigorously" (*Peter Kalm's Travels in North America: The English Version of 1770*, ed. Adolph B. Benson [New York, 1937], II, 614).

52. William B. Hamilton, "The Post Revolutionary War South, 1783–1805," in *Travels in the Old South*, ed. Clark, II, 75.

53. Miranda, *Travels*, 58.

54. "I forgot to mention Mrs. Washington's sweet little grandchildren, who, [I] imagine, will come in for a share of the General's fortune, with the Major [George Augustine Washington]. I fancy he is worth £100,000 sterling, and lives at the rate of three or four thousand a year—always keeping a genteel table for strangers that almost daily visit him, as a thing of course" (Hunter, *Quebec to Carolina*, 197).

55. Visitors from Catholic countries demonstrated considerable interest in the Quakers and their meetings (see Miranda, *Travels*, 53–54; Castiglioni, *Viaggio*, II, 33–38; Jacques Pierre Brissot de Warville, *Nouveau voyage dans les États-Unis de l'Amérique Septentrionale, fait en 1788* [3 vols., Paris, 1791], I, 283–93; Vidua, *Lettere*, III, 52).

56. Chastellux, *Travels*, I, 144–45. Count Francesco Arese, a Milanese nobleman who visited Philadelphia in 1837, wrote of the "National Museum": "There were a few dozen stones, a few dozen portraits of men who deserved much better, some bad animals who were not stuffed badly enough to be scorned by rats and worms, an old Arabian room, Indian costumes, a Mexican sabre, and a French helmet taken from the battlefield of Waterloo and covered with a large label" (Lynn M. Case, "Philadelphia and Baltimore in 1837," *Pennsylvania Magazine of History and Biography*, LVII [1933], 185). For a more favorable account of the museum, see Charles William Janson, *The Stranger in America, 1793–1806*, ed. Carl S. Driver (New York, 1935), 197–200.

57. An exception was Barbé-Marbois, who wrote: "But the garden! . . . It was in a state of neglect which caused us actual pain" (*Letters*, 132).

58. *Ibid.*, 70–71.

59. Castiglioni reported that Arthur Middleton, who had traveled in Europe, had "una discreta quantità di buone pitture" (*Viaggio*, I, 234). "Hunting, dancing, and smoking tobacco in pipes are favorite diversions. Society is not very animated in the city, despite the fact that there is no lack of educated and knowledgeable persons" (Miranda, *Travels*, 23).

60. Edwin M. Stone, *Our French Allies, . . . in the Great War of the American Revolution from 1778 to 1782* (Providence, 1884), 257–64. See also Castiglioni, *Viaggio*, II, 97–98; Miranda, *Travels*, 137–42; Hunter, *Quebec to Carolina*, 121–25.

Notes to Section 2. The Middle States and New England

1. Prior to the Revolution the Common Council of the city of New York granted valuable riparian rights to private persons, in particular to members of the Council. The city, however, retained and developed some important water-front property which it leased for a term of years to the highest bidder. Profits arising from the use of the docks belonged to the lessee (George William Edwards, *New York as an Eighteenth Century Municipality, 1731–1776* [Columbia University Studies in History, Economics and Public Law, LXXV, No. 2; New York, 1917], 149–59).

2. Probably Anthony Stewart, a Loyalist who was at New York in July 1783. He, with fifty-four others, petitioned for grants of land in Nova Scotia (Lorenzo Sabine, *The American Loyalists* [Boston, 1847], 632). Perhaps Alexander Stewart of the firm of A. Stewart and Company, 68 Wall Street; his residence was on Garden Street (Joseph A. Scoville [Walter Barrett], *The Old Merchants of New York City* [New York, 1862], V, 110). Or James Stewart, a Loyalist, dealer in dry goods (*New York City during the American Revolution, Being a Collection of Original Papers . . . from the Manuscripts in the Possession of the New York Mercantile Library Association* [New York, 1861], 135n.; *Stewart Clan Magazine*, XXVIII [June, 1951], 149–51).

3. Fort George and Lower Battery. Early in 1790 the legislature authorized the demolition of Fort George (I. N. Phelps Stokes, *The Iconography of Manhattan Island, 1498–1909* [New York, 1915–28], I, plates 40, 50, and p. 381).

4. Probably Fraunces' Tavern. Originally the home of Etienne de Lancey, who built it in 1719, it was purchased by Samuel Fraunces in 1762 and converted into a tavern the following year. The "Long Room," to which Dal Verme was doubtless referring, was used for concerts and other entertainments (Lathrop, *Early American Inns and Taverns*, 37–39).

5. The Harlem River ended and the Spuyten Duyvil Creek (Spikendevil Creek) began at Kingsbridge (*Historic New York, Being the First Series of the Half Moon Papers*, ed. Maud W. Goodwin, et al. [New York, 1899], 260–61; for a view of Manhattan Island and Kingsbridge in 1782, see Stokes, *Iconography*, I, plate 50).

6. In 1771 the population of New York City was 21,863. At the end of the Revolution it was probably less than that number. The census of 1786 showed a population of 23,614 (Sidney I. Pomerantz, *New York: An American City, 1783–1803* [New York, 1938], 21; Stokes, *Iconography*, I, 331, V, 1207).

7. The fires of Sept. 21–23, 1776, and of Aug. 3, 1778, caused heavy property losses and much distress among the poor. The first and more destructive of the two fires broke out near Whitehall Slip and spread northward up Broadway and Broad Street destroying virtually all of the buildings between Broadway and the Hudson River as far as St. Paul's

Church, which was saved. Trinity Church and the Lutheran church were burned. The second conflagration destroyed over sixty dwellings and many stores near the water front. Despite rumors of arson, the cause of these fires was probably accidental. Fire hazards, such as the storing of hay and straw in barracks, were numerous, and fire prevention regulations as well as fire-fighting equipment were inadequate (Stokes, *Iconography*, I, 324, 333–34; Edwards, *New York*, 128–41).

8. "The chair was a two-wheeled vehicle with a seat for two, and sometimes with an additional small seat, almost over the shafts for the driver" (Dunbar, *Travel in America*, I, 46).

9. Brig. Gen. Samuel Birch (Oscar T. Barck, Jr., *New York City during the War for Independence with Special Reference to the Period of British Occupation* [New York, 1931], 53).

10. New York *Royal Gazette*, July 2, 1763.

11. Elias Boudinot, the President of Congress, reported to Washington on June 21 that the mutinous troops had entered Philadelphia on the previous day "in a very orderly manner" and taken possession of the barracks. Four or five hundred men were involved in the mutiny. The leaders were "a Mr. Carbery a deranged officer, and a Mr. Sullivan a Lieutenant of Horse, both of whom made their escape." On June 21, Congress resolved that "the President on the advice of the committee be authorized and directed to summon the members of Congress to meet on Thursday next at Trenton or Princeton in New Jersey" (*Letters of Members of the Continental Congress*, ed. Edmund C. Burnett [Washington, D.C., 1921–36], VII, 193–94, 195–96; James Madison to Edmund Randolph, June 30, 1783, *ibid.*, VII, 207–8; *Journals of the Continental Congress*, ed. Worthington C. Ford et al. [Washington, D.C., 1904–37], XXIV, 410).

12. The comedy was *The West Indian*, the farce, *The Cheats of Scapin*, both presented by the Dennis Ryan Company. The band was directed by Signor Gaetano Franceschini. Military bands were considered superior to those of regular theatrical companies. The John Street Theatre, where these performances were held, stood on the north side of John Street between Broadway and Nassau Street. The theatre first opened in 1767 and finally closed in 1798 (New York *Royal Gazette*, July 2, 1783; George C. D. Odell, *Annals of the New York Stage* [New York, 1927], I, 111–13, 226–27; Stokes, *Iconography*, I, 382–83).

13. The British troops were recalled from Kingsbridge when New York was evacuated by the British, Nov. 25, 1783 (Stokes, *Iconography*, I, 330).

14. Fort Washington, renamed Fort Knyphausen by the British (for a brief description of these fortifications, dominated by Fort Washington, see Benson J. Lossing, *The Pictorial Field-Book of the Revolution* [New York, 1860], II, 610n.; John A. Kouwenhoven, *The Columbia Historical Portrait of New York* [New York, 1953], 71–72; Wilbur C. Abbott, *New York in the Revolution* [Port Washington, N.Y., 1962], 202–4; Stokes, *Iconography*, I, plate 46 [map by Claude Joseph Sauthier]).

15. This was the Collect, or Fresh Water Pond (Stokes, *Iconography*, I, plates 40, 58, and pp. 430–33).

16. Schoepf stated that the "Flying Machine" carried from ten to twelve

passengers. The vehicle probably had four benches, three of which were in the interior, and could accommodate nine passengers. The "Flying Machines" advertised their services (Schoepf, *Travels*, I, 42–43; Earle, *Stage-Coach and Tavern Days*, 262; *New York Gazette and Weekly Mercury*, July 7, 1783; Dunbar, *History of Travel*, I, 180–86).

17. Elias Boudinot of New Jersey served as President of Congress from Nov. 4, 1782, to Nov. 3, 1783. Congress began to meet in Princeton on June 26 following the mutiny of the Pennsylvania troops during the previous week.

18. The fireworks had been delayed because of rain. Francesco dal Verme to Antonio dal Verme, July 12, 1783, Dal Verme Archives (see p. 39).

19. The library room on the second floor of Nassau Hall in which Congress met no longer exists. There were probably forty students at the college (George Adams Boyd, *Elias Boudinot, Patriot and Statesman, 1740–1821* [Princeton, N.J., 1952], 127–37).

20. The famous orrery which David Rittenhouse built for the College of New Jersey was completed in February 1771. The British prevented any damage being done to the orrery by posting a sentry at the door of the room where it was kept. Responsibility for injuring the machinery of the planetarium very likely rests on the Continental troops who occupied Nassau Hall following its evacuation by the British (Brooke Hindle, *David Rittenhouse* [Princeton, N.J., 1964], 85–88; Thomas J. Wertenbaker, *Princeton, 1746–1896* [Princeton, N.J., 1946], 60–61).

21. The American troops stationed at Princeton probably committed more vandalism than did the British (William A. Dod, *History of the College of New Jersey, From Its Commencement, A.D., 1746, to 1783* [Princeton, N.J., 1844], 46; Willard Thorp, ed., *The Lives of Eighteen from Princeton* [Princeton, N.J., 1946], 79).

22. Boudinot was living at Morven, an estate on the outskirts of Princeton (Boyd, *Elias Boudinot*, 11, 126, 129).

23. "This cataract [Passaic or Totowa Falls], which is 72 feet high and 350 feet wide, is the first thing that stirs the curiosity of almost all foreigners; it is only 18 miles from New York. . . . The inn of this region is one of the best in the land" (Michel-Guillaume St. Jean de Crèvecoeur, *Journey into Northern Pennsylvania and the State of New York*, trans. Clarissa S. Bostelmann [Ann Arbor, Mich., 1964], 601). Bellano, at the mouth of the Pioverna River, is on the eastern side of Lake Como.

24. Barbé-Marbois, Secretary of the French Legation in Philadelphia, wrote of this move: "It was extremely important for the Americans to shut off this river [Hudson]. . . . To stop the enemy they have put in a huge chain which crosses the river and is stoutly moored to the two banks. . . . The place where West Point is, is happily chosen. The river narrows at that spot, and since it curves on itself, the headway of a ship which arrives with full sail, or pushed by the tide, is almost destroyed" (*Letters*, 117).

25. General Knox was in command of West Point, Verplanck, Stony Point, and Dobbs Ferry. His headquarters were in a large stone house which has been preserved (North Callahan, *Henry Knox, General Washington's General* [New York, 1958], 195–97).

26. Washington's headquarters at Newburgh were in the Jonathan Hasbrouck house, which is still standing.

27. Boudinot wrote to Washington, July 8: "This will be handed to your Excellency by the Count Del Vermé, a nobleman of Milan in Italy—By means of his Cousin Prince Caraminici an Ambassador at the Court of London, he was recommended by the Duke of Portland to Dr. Franklin, Mr. Laurens & Mr. Adams, who have warmly addressed this illustrious Traveller to the Notice of Congress—Permit me Sir to request your kind attention [to] the Count on his Visit at Head Quarters—His design is to make a Tour through the united States, and to see the principle men of each State" (Washington Papers, CCXXIII, 30, Lib. Cong.). On July 16, Washington wrote to the President of Congress that he had decided "to wear away a little Time, in performing a Tour to the Northward, as far as Tyconderoga and Crown point, and perhaps as far up the Mohawk River as fort Schuyler" (*Writings of Washington*, ed. Fitzpatrick, XXVII, 68–70).

28. "The Winter-Cantonment of the American Army and its Vicinity for 1783," Erskine-Dewitt Map, No. 1, New York Historical Society Library, shows the arrangement of the camp. The "Sala," called the Temple, was a one-story building of roughhewn logs, probably 80 ft. long and 40 ft. wide (Lossing, *Field-Book*, I, 685–86).

29. The two deputies from Albany were Abraham Schuyler and Leonard Gansevoort, Jr. Their letter read: "The Corporation of the City of Albany having been apprized of your Excellency's being on your way to that Place, have deputed us as a Committee to meet your Excellency previous to your arrival—we have come thus far for that Purpose and are at the House of Mr. Gerrit Staats where we would request your Excellency's Presence for a few Moments" (Washington Papers, CCXXIII, 79, Lib. Cong.).

30. Abraham Ten Broeck was mayor of Albany. Johannes Jacobse Beeckman served as the twenty-ninth mayor of the town from June 27, 1783, to Oct. 8, 1786 (Cuyler Reynolds, *Albany Chronicles: A History of the City Arranged Chronologically* [Albany, 1906], 810). The drawings of early Albany executed by James Eights (Albany Institute of History and Art) show the Dutch influence on the architecture of this town. Particularly interesting are the views of North Pearl Street (see Helen W. Reynolds, *Dutch Houses in the Hudson Valley before 1776* [New York, 1929]).

31. The Schuyler mansion, orginally called The Pastures, has been restored as it was in the 18th century (Anna K. Cunningham, *Schuyler Mansion: A Critical Catalogue of the Furnishings and Decorations* [Albany, 1955]; Harold D. Eberlein, *Manors and Historical Homes of the Hudson Valley* [Philadelphia, 1924], 222–36; Harold D. Eberlein and Cortlandt Van Dyke Hubbard, *Historic Houses of the Hudson Valley* [New York, 1942], 133–41).

32. One of the daughters was Mrs. Elizabeth Schuyler Hamilton, wife of Alexander Hamilton, who was then serving in Congress. The other daughter was Mrs. Angelica Schuyler Church (Carter). The remarkable Indian may have been Louis Atyataghronghta, a chief of the friendly Oneida tribe and a person of influence in the Caughnawaga tribe, one of the Seven

Nations in Canada. Louis acted as agent for the Americans in their efforts to win the support of the Canadian Indians to the Revolutionary cause. In recognition for his distinctive services on the New York frontier, Congress commissioned him a lieutenant colonel in 1779. In 1782 the War Office commended him for "his interest with the Tribes, his sagacity, integrity, and firm attachment to the cause of the United States." Louis was reputed to have been of French, Indian, and Negro descent (Burnett, ed., *Letters,* VII, 231–32; Chastellux, *Travels,* 198, 288n.; Lossing, *Field-Book,* I, 280, 281n.; James Dean to Schuyler, Sept. 18, 1783, Schuyler Papers, New York Public Library; Papers of the Continental Congress, No. 42, VIII, fols. 83–86, No. 78, VII, fols. 243, 244, XIV, fol. 489, No. 147, III, fols. 173, 175, 391, No. 149, I, fols. 473–76, National Archives).

33. Cohoes Falls. Governor Thomas Pownall also estimated its height at 70 ft. ("A View of the Great Cohoes Falls, on the Mohawk River; the Fall about Seventy feet; the River near a Quarter of a Mile broad. Sketch'd on the Spot by his Excellency Governor Pownal," painted by Paul Sandby, engraved by William Elliott [London, 1761], New York Historical Society). The cataract was a favorite tourist attraction and a source of inspiration to artists, including John Trumbull and William Dunlap (Theodore Sizer, *The Works of Colonel John Trumbull, Artist of the American Revolution* [New Haven, 1950], plate 40; *Diary of William Dunlap (1766–1839)* [New York Historical Society Collections, LXII–LXIV; New York, 1930], I, xxiii).

34. The first battle at Freeman's Farm was fought on Sept. 19, 1777. The third house built by Schuyler at Saratoga is still standing. The first one was burned by the French in 1745, the second one by the British in 1777. According to local tradition, house number three was built by American troops in seventeen days (Christopher Ward, *The War of the Revolution,* ed. John R. Alden [New York, 1952], II, 504–12; John H. Brandow, *The Story of Old Saratoga* [Albany, 1919], 323–31; Eberlein and Hubbard, *Houses of the Hudson Valley,* plate 126).

35. The sawmills belonged to General Schuyler. He also kept a store at Saratoga (Don R. Gerlach, *Philip Schuyler and the American Revolution, 1733–1777* [Lincoln, Neb., 1964], 53–58; Brandow, *Saratoga,* 290–91; Chastellux, *Travels,* I, 218, 354n.).

36. The Oneidas and Tuscaroras supported the American cause. The refusal of the Oneidas to aid the British weakened the Iroquois Confederacy. When the Tuscaroras emigrated from North Carolina after 1713 they settled in New York. Although they were admitted into the Five Nations —Cayuga, Seneca, Mohawk, Onondaga, Oneida—which thus became the Six Nations, the Tuscaroras had no independent territory (Lewis H. Morgan, *League of the Ho De-No-Sau-Nee or Iroquois* [New York, 1901], I, 26–28, II, 195–96; *Census of the State of New-York for 1855* [Albany, 1857], 510–11, 513–14).

37. On the conduct of the Iroquois toward female captives La Rochefoucauld-Liancourt wrote that the greatest crime among the Indians was to touch a captive, even with her consent. This crime would be immediately punished with death. But as soon as the captive was set at liberty, there existed no further prohibition, provided she consented (François Alex-

andre F. duc de La Rochefoucauld-Liancourt, *Voyage dans les États-Unis d'Amérique, fait en 1795, 1796 et 1797* [8 vols., Paris, 1799], I, 307–8).

38. Fort Edward, built by Phineas [or Phinehas] Lyman of Connecticut, was originally called Fort Lyman. Sir William Johnson renamed it Fort Edward for Edward Augustus, Duke of York and Albany. The fort was razed in 1775. Washington's party probably halted at the Red House, a large two-story building (William H. Hill, *Old Fort Edward* [Fort Edward, 1929], 17, 86, 248–49, 253).

39. Below Glens Falls many fossils embedded in the rocks could be seen. The most remarkable petrification, called the Big Snake, resembled a large serpent lying on the surface of a flat rock (Lossing, *Field-Book*, I, 104–5).

40. Washington had made arrangements for the delivery of these boats to Lake George (Washington to Philip Schuyler and to Lt. Henry Dimler, July 15, 1783, *Writings of Washington*, ed. Fitzpatrick, XXVII, 65–67). Fort George, a weak post at the head of Lake George sometimes called Fort William Henry, was destroyed by Montcalm in 1757 (Thomas Jones, *History of New York during the Revolutionary War* [New York, 1879], I, 200, 550; Benson J. Lossing, *The Empire State* [Hartford, 1888], 165–67; for a sketch of this and some other forts visited by Dal Verme, see "A Set of Plans and Forts in America. Reduced from Actual Surveys, 1765," photostats in New York Historical Society).

41. Sir William Johnson renamed Lac St. Sacrament Lake George, in honor of King George II (Lossing, *Empire State*, 165–66).

42. See Stephen H. Pell, *Fort Ticonderoga* (Fort Ticonderoga Museum, 1946).

43. The fortifications at Crown Point were in such state of ruin in 1776 that they were considered indefensible (Ward, *War of the Revolution*, I, 384–87).

44. The mosquitoes in this area were indeed troublesome. Wrote Peter Kalm: "I never saw the *mosquitoes* more plentiful in any part of America than they are here. They were so eager for our blood that we could not rest all night, though we had surrounded ourselves with fire" (*Travels*, I, 365).

45. A temporary bower built by the soldiers at West Point accommodated more than 500 people (Douglas S. Freeman, *George Washington* [New York, 1948–57], V, 416 and n.).

46. Before setting out on his tour of upper New York, Washington instructed Steuben to go to Canada to negotiate with Gen. Frederick Haldimand for the possession of the posts which were to be ceded by Great Britain in accordance with Article VII of the provisional Anglo-American peace treaty. Steuben was also ordered to inspect the frontier forts as far westward as Detroit and to report on their military value to the United States (Instructions to Steuben, July 12, 1783, *Writings of Washington*, ed. Fitzpatrick, XXVII, 61–63).

47. Burgoyne ordered the destruction of the buildings because they served as cover for the American troops during the Battle of Saratoga (Lossing, *Field-Book*, I, 73–74).

48. In the South these drinks were called "antifogmatics" (John Ber-

The Middle States and New England 109

nard, *Retrospections of America, 1797-1811* [New York, 1887], 206).

49. Schuyler cut a road from Saratoga to High Rock Spring in 1783. Sir William Johnson is reputed to have been the first white man to visit the springs and to have recognized their medicinal properties. Washington and Gov. George Clinton contemplated making a joint purchase of the springs (Brandow, *Saratoga*, 331-35; Richard L. Allen, *An Analysis of the Principal Mineral Fountains at Saratoga Springs* [New York, 1858], 14-16; Washington to Clinton, Nov. 25, 1784, *Writings of Washington*, ed. Fitzpatrick, 500-503).

50. The conical rock which contained the water of High Rock Spring attracted wide attention. In 1809 the ash-colored cone measured five feet in height and nine feet at the base; the opening was nearly ten inches in diameter and the water rose to within two feet of the top. In 1825 the height was estimated at between five and six feet; the water remained two feet below the circular opening which was then nearly twelve inches in diameter. The rock was cracked, possibly by a falling tree, sometime after 1783. This may account for the cessation of the periodic overflow of the water and the maintenance of the height of the cone at around five feet, only two feet higher than it was in 1783 (Valentine Seaman, *A Dissertation on the Mineral Waters of Saratoga* [New York, 1809], 26-31; John H. Steel, *An Analysis of the Mineral Waters of Saratoga and Ballston* [Saratoga Springs, 1825], 72-75).

51. The effervescent water was carried away daily, sometimes for a distance of eight or ten miles. Dough made with this water was reported to be immediately ready for the oven. A well-raised cake could be made in half an hour (Seaman, *Mineral Waters of Saratoga*, 36-40).

52. Local tradition had it that when Washington's party lost their way the General twice asked for directions from one "Tom" Conner who was chopping wood at his cabin door. On the second inquiry Tom is said to have replied: "I tell you, turn back and take the first right-hand path into the woods, and then stick to it—any darned fool would know the way!" When Tom learned that the dignified spokesman was none other than Washington he was greatly mortified at having given so uncivil an answer. For this he was ever afterwards joshed by his neighbors. Gen. James Gordon was living on the Middle Line Road. When the distinguished party left for Schenectady, Gordon accompanied them for some distance (William L. Stone, *Reminiscences of Saratoga and Ballston* [New York, 1880], 13-16; J. H. French, *Gazetteer of New York* [Syracuse, N.Y., 1860], 587n.).

53. This long and poorly composed memorial was written July 25, 1783, at Schenectady, where the friendly Indians had sought refuge following the destruction of their villages by the British in 1780. In pathetic detail the Indians described their grievances and begged Washington, as "the head Warriour of the thirteen United States," to intervene in their behalf (Washington Papers, CCXXIII, 95a, 95b, Lib. Cong.).

54. Fort Van Rensselaer (Canajoharie) was the headquarters of Col. Marinus Willett (1740-1830), who distinguished himself in the border warfare of New York (Ward, *War of the Revolution*, II, 650-52;

William M. Willett, *A Narrative of the Military Actions of Colonel Marinus Willett Taken Chiefly from His Own Manuscript* [New York, 1831]).

55. Several small forts were built at Canajoharie and afforded some protection against Indian incursions (French, *Gazetteer of New York State*, 412 and n.).

56. The large stockaded house of Gen. Nicholas Herkimer at German Flats was called Fort Herkimer. Nearby Fort Dayton was a small blockhouse. German Flats, settled by Palatines, was attacked during the French and Indian War and the Revolution. Fortunately there were several stone buildings in the village, including the church, which afforded protection to the inhabitants. Herkimer family tradition has preserved some sentimental details of Washington's visit (*ibid.*, 342n., 344; Ward, *War of the Revolution*, II, 488–90, 633, 650–52; Phoebe Strong Cowen, *The Herkimers and Schuylers* [Albany, 1903], 8–39).

57. Washington wasted no time in correcting the deplorable condition of the roads and waterways in this area. On his return to Albany he instructed Col. Marinus Willett to repair the bridges from Fort Herkimer to Fort Schuyler and to improve water communication to Lake Oneida. From Newburgh he reported to the President of Congress that the land route to western New York was for the present "impracticable" and the water route "extremely difficult . . . as the River is very much obstructed with fallen and floating trees from the long disuse of the navigation" (Aug. 4 and 6, 1783, *Writings of Washington*, ed. Fitzpatrick, XXVII, 79–80, 84–86).

58. Fort Schuyler, called Fort Stanwix before the Revolution, was constructed in 1758. Here in 1768 Sir William Johnson negotiated a treaty with the Iroquois in which the Indians ceded to the English their rights to a large area extending from central New York southward to the Kentucky frontier. In 1777 the fort was made sufficiently defensible to withstand an investment by a strong force of British regulars, Loyalists, German mercenaries, and Indians under the command of Col. Barry St. Leger. In 1781 Fort Schuyler was destroyed by flood and fire (Ward, *War of the Revolution*, II, 482–91; French, *Gazetteer of New York*, 461).

59. Fort Stanwix or Schuyler, on the site of present Rome, N.Y., was only a mile from Wood Creek which ran into Lake Oneida (see Crèvecoeur, *Journey*, trans. Bostelmann, 177, 592; John W. Barber and Henry Howe, *Historical Collections of the State of New York* [New York, 1844], 374; Noble E. Whitford, "The Canal System and Its Influences," in *History of the State of New York*, ed. Alexander C. Flick [New York, 1933–37], V, 297–305).

60. Probably Joseph Herkimer (b. 1751) (Cowan, *Herkimers and Schuylers*, 111).

61. The village of Cherry Valley was plundered and burned in 1778 by a combined force of Loyalists and Indians under the command of Capt. Walter Butler and Joseph Brant. Washington and his party were probably the guests of Samuel Campbell (Ward, *War of the Revolution*, II, 634–35; William W. Campbell, *Annals of Tryon County* [New York, 1924], 185–91).

The Middle States and New England

62. Canajoharie (Fort Rensselaer). The inhabitants of Tryon County delivered a congratulatory address to Washington in which they referred to their losses during the Revolution. In his reply the General said that his tour had enabled him to observe the "severe distress" of these frontiersmen caused by the "cruel devastations of the enemy." The ravages in Tryon County were indeed impressive: 700 buildings burned; 354 forced to leave their homes; 1,200 farms uncultivated; 197 persons killed; 121 taken prisoners (Washington Papers, CCXXIII, 113, 114, Lib. Cong.; French, *Gazetteer of New York*, 411n.).

63. The Baroness Hyde de Neuville (*ca.* 1779–1849) executed some drawings of the New York Indians. Two of them, in particular, "Mary, Squaw of the Oneida Tribe" and "Indian Family," show the Indians as Dal Verme described them (New York Historical Society Library, Nos. 207, 215).

64. Washington's letters introducing the "Count dal Vermé, an Italian Nobleman of Family and distinction," were addressed to Govs. Jonathan Trumbull, William Greene, Meshech Weare, and to Gen. John Sullivan, John Langdon, and Nathaniel Tracy. The letter to Tracy, a man of substance, contained the following request: "Should he [Dal Verme] stand in need of Money, be so good as to advance it to him, & his Bills will be immediately paid" (Washington Papers, CCXXIII, 122, Lib. Cong.).

65. The congratulatory addresses presented to Gen. Washington and Gov. Clinton had been intended for delivery at the time of their arrival at Albany, July 19, not of their departure, Aug. 4. The former date is crossed out in the address to Washington, which is signed by Abraham Ten Broeck, Mayor. Washington did not reach Newburgh until the afternoon of Aug. 5 (Washington Papers, CCXXIII, 118, Lib. Cong.; Washington's reply in *ibid.*, 119; *The Public Papers of George Clinton* [New York and Albany, 1899–1914], VIII, 230–31).

66. Probably John Tayler or Taylor (1742–1829), merchant, lieutenant governor, and governor of New York. Morgan Lewis (1754–1844), Quartermaster General of the Northern Army under Gates. (*The National Cyclopaedia of American Biography*, XI, 349; Julia Delafield, *Biographies of Francis Lewis and Morgan Lewis* [New York, 1877]).

67. Francisco de Miranda, who visited the arsenal at Springfield in 1784, wrote: "Two wooden warehouses contain seventy-five hundred muskets of French make, some ancient weapons of the same type as was used when the war began, about ninety bronze artillery pieces . . . , two thirteen-inch mortars, four or six twelve-inch cannons, some howitzers and miscellaneous artillery, and carriages, limbers, etc. The powder is kept in a brick warehouse" (Miranda, *Travels*, 113–14; Mason A. Green, *Springfield, 1636–1886: History of a Town and City* [Springfield, Mass., 1888], 285–86; *Journals of Continental Congress*, XXV, 738).

68. The General Court of Massachusetts passed an absurdly strict blue law in 1782. It stipulated that "no Person shall recreate, disport, or unnecessarily walk, or loitre, or assemble, themselves in the Streets, Lanes, Wharves, Highways, common Fields, Pastures, or Orchards of any Town or place." The wardens, who were charged with the execution of the law, were required "to examine all Persons suspected as unnecessarily Travelling . . .

and to demand of all such Persons the Cause thereof, together with their Names and Places of abode." These officials were to carry "a white Wand, not less than seven Feet in Length, as a Badge of his Office." According to Samuel Breck's amusing account of his encounter with a warden, this law was still in effect in 1791. Castiglioni had to stop at Newburyport (*Acts and Laws, Passed by the Great and General Court or Assembly of the Commonwealth of Massachusetts* . . . , Chap. VI, 177–82; *Recollections of Samuel Breck with Passages from His Note-Books, 1771–1862*, ed. H. E. Scudder [Philadelphia, 1877], 179–80; Castiglioni, *Viaggio*, I, 43–44).

69. Philippe-André-Joseph de Létombe was consul general of France for New Hampshire, Massachusetts, Rhode Island, and Connecticut (John Russell Bartlett, ed., *Records of the State of Rhode Island and Providence Plantations in New England* [Providence, 1856–65], IX, 724–25). Dr. Samuel Cooper (1725–1783), clergyman, for many years pastor of the Brattle Square Church. Lt. Gov. Thomas Cushing (1725–88).

70. The beacon, erected on Beacon Hill in 1768, was blown down in 1789. The tall mast was supported by braces and was ascended by means of nails driven into it. An iron frame suspended from an iron crane near the top of the mast held the receptacle containing the combustible material (Samuel A. Drake, *Old Landmarks and Historic Personages of Boston* [Boston, 1900], 349; Breck, *Recollections*, 33–34).

71. The houses in Charlestown had been built chiefly of wood (Lossing, *Field-Book*, I, 544–45).

72. The fort was called the Castle (Drake, *Old Landmarks*, 24, 115).

73. Probably Abiel Smith, whose wife was socially ambitious (Breck, *Recollections*, 191–92; Drake, *Old Landmarks*, 196).

74. The Portsmouth house of Col. Jonathan Warner stands at the corner of Daniels and Chapel Streets. It was built early in the eighteenth century (Mary H. Northend, *Historic Homes of New England* [Boston, 1914], 119–29; Federal Writers' Project, W.P.A., *New Hampshire* [Boston, 1938], 237–38).

75. John Hancock as well as Washington wrote to John Langdon (1741–1819) in behalf of Dal Verme. The beautiful Mrs. Langdon, almost twenty years younger than her husband, was the former Elizabeth Sherburne. Langdon was a successful merchant, soldier, legislator, and chief executive of New Hampshire (Alfred Langdon Elwyn, ed., *Letters by Washington, Adams, Jefferson, and Others, Written during and after the Revolution, to John Langdon, New Hampshire* [Philadelphia, 1880], 61–62; Lawrence Shaw Mayo, *John Langdon of New Hampshire* [Concord, N.H., 1937], 140–41).

76. The Old North Church was built in 1712. John Langdon had a spacious pew in the southeast corner of the church (Charles W. Brewster, *Rambles about Portsmouth*, 1st ser. [Portsmouth, 1873], 326–31).

77. The Assembly Hall on the second floor of the once spacious Assembly House was used for dances, as was the arched hall on the third floor of the Elijah Hall mansion (Federal Writers' Project, W.P.A., *New Hampshire*, 241; Brewster, *Rambles about Portsmouth*, 1st ser., 315–17).

78. Several fortifications were constructed at the outbreak of the Revolution under the direction of Gen. John Sullivan (Washington to Sullivan,

The Middle States and New England 113

Nov. 7, 1775, *Writings of Washington,* ed. Fitzpatrick, IV, 70–71; Charles W. Brewster, *Rambles about Portsmouth,* 2d ser. [Portsmouth, N.H., 1869], 168–70).

79. James Sheafe (1755–1829), prominent merchant, member of the New Hampshire legislature and Executive Council and of the U.S. Congress (*National Cyclopaedia of American Biography,* II, 10). William Whipple (1730–85), merchant and jurist, was one of the signers of the Declaration of Independence.

80. Probably William Wetmore (Drake, *Old Landmarks,* 389; Miranda, *Travels,* 188–89).

81. Probably James Sullivan (1744–86), statesman. Col. Isaac Sears (1730–86), merchant, privateersman, and patriot (Esther Forbes, *Paul Revere & the World He Lived In* [Boston, 1942], 323, 326). The family of William Deblois, a Loyalist sympathizer. His daughter was "esteemed the belle of Boston" and was an accomplished musician (Douglas S. Robertson, ed., *An Englishman in America, 1785, Being the Diary of Joseph Hadfield* [Toronto, 1933], 191).

82. Doctor James Lloyd was a prominent physician and moderate Loyalist. Betsey, Nancy, and Peggy Hunter were renowned for their exceptional beauty and talent. Betsey, who played the harpsichord and sang Italian and French songs, became blind. After his return to Milan, Dal Verme recalled how she sang the "arias of Metastasio" and how generously she gave encores of "General Washington's March." Their mother, Mrs. Deborah Hunter, was the widow of the anatomist, Dr. William Hunter (*Appleton's Cyclopaedia of American Biography,* III, 749; undated letter of Francesco dal Verme, Dal Verme Archives; Mary Ellen Loughrey, *France and Rhode Island, 1686–1800* [New York, 1944], 128; Miranda, *Travels* 142; Hunter, *Quebec to Carolina,* 121).

83. Rainsford Island was the quarantine ground (Drake, *Old Landmarks,* 188).

84. The French battleship which was grounded in 1782 on entering the Narrows was the *Magnifique* (Samuel E. Morison, *John Paul Jones* [Boston, 1959], 318–30).

85. The press reported that the fire consumed a barn and its hay, four horses, and all the horse tackle; the house of a Mr. Russell, together with hay, carriages, and five horses; and the large store of the Hon. William Phillips. The Engine Company of Roxbury helped to put out the fire (Boston, *Continental Journal and Weekly Advertiser,* Aug. 28, 1783). A fire bucket is shown in *Letters and Diary of John Rowe, Boston Merchant,* ed. Anne R. Cunningham (Boston, 1903), opp. p. 74.

86. James Swan resided in the mansion formerly owned by Stephen Greenleaf (Drake, *Old Landmarks,* 313).

87. At the time of Dal Verme's visit, Molliere had a small estate near Charlestown and was engaged to marry one of the daughters of Sears (undated letter of Francesco dal Verme, Dal Verme Archives).

88. On this day the "good subjects" of Louis XVI residing in Boston celebrated the feast of St. Louis at the home of Col. Marston. The "elegant" and "convivial" occasion was marred only by the absence of Létombe, who they supposed was in the country relaxing "from his numerous avocations."

Actually the Consul had gone on the excursion described by Dal Verme, as the press later reported (Boston, *Independent Chronicle and the Universal Advertiser,* Aug. 28, Sept. 4, 1783; *Providence Gazette and Country Journal,* Sept. 6, 1783).

89. Samuel Breck (1747 o.s.–1809) was a prominent merchant and a member of the Massachusetts House of Representatives (Breck, *Recollections,* 17–29).

90. Nathaniel Tracy, who with his brother had been very successful in privateering, lived in the celebrated Craigie house at Cambridge, which had been Washington's headquarters and which became the home of Henry W. Longfellow (Breck, *Recollections,* 25–31; Northend, *Historic Homes,* 100–103).

91. Benjamin Hitchbourn had bought the Dorchester estate of Andrew Oliver, a Tory. Hitchbourn's accidental (?) shooting of Benjamin Andrews and his subsequent marriage to the handsome widow engendered endless gossip (Forbes, *Paul Revere,* 347–48, 370).

92. Jabez Bowen (1739–1815), deputy gov. of Rhode Island, 1778–86, and chancellor of Brown University, 1785–1815 (*National Cyclopaedia of American Biography,* VIII, 29; Stone, *French Allies,* 239–43, 246–49).

93. The press reported that the "Gentlemen of the Corporation" convened at the College at 9 A.M., and from there walked in procession to the meetinghouse, preceded by the students and the candidates for the first degree. The program consisted of music, orations, a forensic disputation, and an address delivered by Dr. James Mann of Harvard. After listing the recipients of degrees and complimenting the musicians, the account added that the Consul General of France and the "Count dal Vermé" had "honored the Corporation" with their company. In the evening "an animating sermon" was preached by the Rev. Samuel Stillman of Boston. An announcement was made that the Corporation of the College had raised a considerable sum of money for the immediate purchase of "a compleat philosophical apparatus" and a large number of books for the Library (*Providence Gazette and Country Journal,* Sept. 6, 1783).

94. The editor is indebted to Mary T. Quinn, Dept. of State, R.I., for information on Chace, a merchant of Providence.

95. Moses Brown (1738–1836), successful businessman and humanitarian. His daughter, Sarah, married William Almy in 1789 (Mack Thompson, *Moses Brown, Reluctant Reformer* [Chapel Hill, N.C., 1962]).

96. "On Thursday Evening there was a Ball at Mr. Hacker's Hall, at which were present the Consul-General of France, the Count dal Vermé, many other respectable Strangers, and a most Splendid Assemblage of Ladies" (*Providence Gazette and Country Journal,* Sept. 6, 1783).

97. Létombe's arrival in Newport was duly noted in the *Newport Mercury,* Sept. 6, 1783.

98. Christopher Champlin (1730–1805), wealthy merchant and banker, had an estate of two thousand acres. Champlin's daughter, Peggy, rivaled the Misses Hunter in beauty. Mrs. Hunter lived on the southeast corner of Thames and Mary Streets (Richard Le Baron Bowen, "John Scott, Merchant," *Rhode Island History,* IV [July, 1945], 89n.; Stone, *Our*

The Middle States and New England 115

French Allies, 257–64; Loughrey, *France and Rhode Island,* 130; Elton M. Manuel, *Merchants and Mansions of Bygone Days* [Newport, R.I., 1939], 25).

99. George Augustine Washington, for whom Dal Verme had a letter from Gen. Washington (*Writings of Washington,* ed. Fitzpatrick, XXVII, 79n.).

100. During the Revolution, Newport's population was greatly reduced and property valued at $624,000 specie was destroyed. Miranda noted that the lack of trees gave "an air of aridity to all the countryside just as one sees in La Mancha of Castile" (Lossing, *Field-Book,* I, 656–57; Miranda, *Travels,* 133–34).

101. The Temple Jeshuat Israel on Touro Street was designed by Peter Harrison, a pupil of Sir Christopher Wren. It combines the classic colonial style with the synagogue architecture of the Spanish-Portuguese Jews. The building was completed in 1762 and dedicated in 1763 (Morris A. Gutstein, *The Story of the Jews of Newport* [New York, 1936], 79–110; Federal Writers' Project, W.P.A., *Rhode Island* [New York, 1937], 219).

102. The 1782 Census of Rhode Island lists Benjamin Brenton, son of Jahleel and Francis (Cranston) Brenton. Benjamin Brenton married Rachel Cooke by whom he had ten children (the editor is indebted to Mary T. Quinn, Dept. of State, R.I., for this information).

103. Fort Griswold, on the left bank of the Thames River opposite New London, was commanded by Lt. Col. William Ledyard. After the unconditional surrender of the fort, Sept. 6, 1781, Ledyard and most of the garrison were massacred by the Tories, Hessians, and British who swarmed into the fort (Lossing, *Field-Book,* I, 609–13).

104. New London and Groton were burned by forces under Benedict Arnold (Ward, *War of the Revolution,* II, 626–28).

105. The Acadians were expelled in 1755. In 1756 small groups of Acadians were distributed among fifty towns in Connecticut, with Norwich and New Haven receiving the largest number, 19. The Acadians could not leave the towns to which they were assigned without proper authorization, but care was taken not to separate families and special provisions were made for the aged and ill. It has been estimated that Connecticut received 108 men, 109 women, and 449 children. In New London the Acadians found employment in construction work (*The Public Records of the Colony of Connecticut,* ed. Charles J. Hoadley [Hartford, 1850–90], X, 425, 452–53; Émile Lauvrière, *La Tragédie d'Un Peuple* [Paris, 1922], I, 161; Florence S. Marcy Crofut, *Guide to the History and the Historic Sites of Connecticut* [New Haven, 1937], II, 547, 729; Arthur G. Doughty, *The Acadian Exiles* [Toronto, 1921], 138–40).

106. Dr. Ezra Stiles (1727–95) was President of Yale College from 1778 until his death. At the inauguration of President Timothy Dwight, Sept. 1795, the College was illuminated by placing eight candles at each window (Franklin B. Dexter, *Student Life at Yale College under the First President Dwight* [Worcester, 1918], 4; Edmund S. Morgan, *The Gentle Puritan: A Life of Ezra Stiles, 1727–1795* [New Haven, 1962], 361–65).

107. This riotous celebration was an early version of "the Calliathump," when students would assemble late at night "armed with horns, drums (if

possible), pans, pails, kettles, and clubs, and thence, after having chosen a leader, . . . [would] sally forth to the revel, making melody of various characters" (Ezekiel P. Belden, *Sketches of Yale College* [New York, 1843], 165–66).

108. The Yale commencement of 1783 was attended by the usual commencement noise, dancing, and violence. President Stiles recorded that 74 squares of glass were broken on college property, chiefly by town fellows, he added (Alexander Cowie, *Educational Problems at Yale College in the Eighteenth Century* [New Haven, 1936], 22; Ezra Stiles, *The Literary Diary of Ezra Stiles,* ed. Franklin B. Dexter [New York, 1901], III, 94n.).

109. Dr. Stiles, who liked academic pomp and ceremony, described the commencement exercises in great detail and listed the recipients of all degrees. "Finally," he wrote "the Deg. of Doctor in Laws was conferred *honoris gratia* upon the illustrious Count *Dal Verme* of Milan, an Italian Nobleman on his Travels through the United States, who did us the honor of his presence: as did the honorable M. *Joseph de Letombe* Consul general of France for the four N Engld States." The learned and gracious President took the time to become acquainted with the recipients of the honorary degrees. "Count Dal Verme was born in Milan," he noted, "he told me he was aet. 24. Young!" The diploma for Dal Verme was not written until Feb. 25, 1784, and was not forwarded until Sept. 11 of that same year (see Appendix II above, p. 91). The commencements were held in the Brick Meetinghouse and were followed by parties at the Statehouse (Stiles, *Diary,* III, 91–94, 113, 137; Rollin G. Osterweis, *Three Centuries of New Haven, 1638–1938* [New Haven, 1953], 175).

110. On July 28, Congress requested Washington to come to Princeton at his earliest convenience. Somewhat reluctantly the General left Newburgh, probably on Aug. 19, and arrived in New Jersey two days later. By Aug. 24 he was at Rocky Hill, lodged at the home of Mrs. Margaret Berrien (*Journals of Continental Congress,* XXIV, 452; *Writings of Washington,* ed. Fitzpatrick, XXVII, 130n.; Freeman, *Washington,* V, 451–52).

111. Anne-César, Chevalier de La Luzerne (1741–91), French Minister to the United States for five years, 1779–84. During his stay in Philadelphia, La Luzerne lived in the house owned by Joshua Carpenter, which had extensive grounds (Carl L. Lokke, comp., *List of United States Diplomatic Representatives, 1778–1820, and List of Foreign Diplomatic Representatives, 1778–1820* [Washington, D.C., 1955], 56; Harold D. Eberlein and Cortlandt J. Hubbard, *Portrait of a Colonial City: Philadelphia, 1670–1838* [Philadelphia, 1939], 9).

112. Probably Robert Morris. The Department of Finance, of which Morris was Superintendent, did not move to Princeton during the summer of 1783 (the President of Congress to Robert Morris, June 30, 1783, Burnett, ed., *Letters,* VII, 205).

113. A compatriot of the Marquis Cesare Beccaria would, of course, visit the penal institution, a noted tourist attraction. For a description of the prison, see La Rochefoucauld-Liancourt, *Voyage,* VI, 244–66.

114. On Sept. 13, 1783, Congress passed an act to pardon Sgts. Christian Nagle and John Morrison, sentenced to die, and "gunner Lilly,"

The Middle States and New England 117

"drummer Horn," Thomas Flowers, and William Carman, sentenced to receive corporal punishment. At the same time Congress thanked Maj. Gen. Robert Howe for the manner in which he had conducted the inquiry (*Journals of Continental Congress,* XXV, 565–67; Samuel Holten to Samuel Adams, Aug. 14, 1783, Burnett, ed., *Letters,* VII, 262–63; *Pennsylvania Journal and the Weekly Advertiser,* Sept. 24, 1783; *Pennsylvania Packet,* Sept. 25, 1783).

115. Perhaps the most distinguished gathering in American academic history witnessed these commencement exercises held in the Presbyterian church at Princeton. First in importance was Gen. Washington, *Pater Patriae.* With him were seven signers of the Declaration of Independence, nine signers of the Articles of Confederation, and eleven future signers of the Constitution of the United States. The Chevalier de La Luzerne was also present. The trustees of the College demonstrated their gratitude for Washington's gift of fifty guineas by requesting him to sit for a picture to be painted by Charles Willson Peale. This portrait hangs in the Faculty Room at Princeton University. The press account of the commencement exercises included the names of the recipients of degrees (Wertenbaker, *Princeton,* 65–66; *Pennsylvania Gazette,* Oct. 8, 1783).

116. Possibly Mr. Smith, an innkeeper and lawyer, mentioned by Chastellux (*Travels,* II, 521).

117. Possibly Lt. Col. Neigal Gray (d. 1786) of the 12th Pennsylvania who was cashiered June 2, 1778 (Francis B. Heitman, *Historical Register of Officers of the Continental Army during the War of the Revolution* [Washington, D.C., 1893], 198).

118. Chastellux has left an account of the warm, if somewhat importunate, hospitality of Robert Hoops. The Frenchman described Belvidere as "small, but neat and handsome." Hoops briefly served as Deputy Commissary of Issues in 1777 (Chastellux, *Travels,* II, 517–22; Heitman, *Historical Register,* 227).

119. Dal Verme was doubtless describing the flying squirrel, *Glaucomys volans,* rather than the *bellora,* a weasel. Flying squirrels do not fly, but go from tree to tree "by gliding with outstretched membranes from an elevated position to a point lower down, usually near the ground." They are nocturnal creatures (Arthur H. Howell, *Revision of the American Flying Squirrels, North American Fauna* No. 44 [Washington, D.C., 1918], 5–24).

120. Nazareth was in the northeastern confines of the Barony of Nazareth. Water from the nearby springs was brought to the town in pipes and distributed through pumps. The Rose Inn at Nazareth was built in 1752. In 1754 it adopted the sign of the rose to perpetuate the Barony's quitrent token—one red rose. Another inn was built in 1771 (George M. Shultz, comp., A. A. Ettinger, ed., *Two Centuries of Nazareth, Pennsylvania* [Nazareth, Pa., 1940], 45; Schoepf, *Travels,* I, 155; Theophile Cazenove, *Cazenove Journal,* ed. Rayner W. Kelsey [Haverford, Pa., 1922], 19–24; Joseph M. Levering, *A History of Bethlehem, Pennsylvania, 1741–1892* [Bethlehem, Pa., 1903], 44n., 257n.; Lathrop, *Inns and Taverns,* 146).

121. This bird was the ruffed grouse or partridge (Chastellux, *Travels,* II, 522, 649).

122. Castiglioni wrote that "Sig. Osley" conducted him around Bethlehem (*Viaggio,* II, 9). The number of curious visitors to Bethlehem probably necessitated the use of a cicerone—*Fremden-Diener,* as he was called—who would invariably take them to the Sisters' House where handiwork was displayed for sale. "The profits of entertaining strangers is very considerable," wrote a somewhat critical visitor, "and conducted with much art the purchases of their little manufactures is at a most extravagant rate" (Joshua Gilpin, "Journey to Bethlehem," *Pa. Mag. of Hist. and Biog.,* XLVI [1922], 150; John Hill Martin, *Historical Sketch of Bethlehem in Pennsylvania, With Some Account of the Moravian Church* [Philadelphia, 1873], 93).

123. William Peter Knolton presented a spinet to the Bethlehem community in 1744. Two years later a small portable organ was made and installed by John Klemm (Levering, *Bethlehem,* 171–72).

124. Moravian evangelism in foreign parts began in 1732 when missionaries were sent to St. Thomas, Virgin Islands, then a colony of Denmark. In the next two years Moravian evangelists went to Greenland, St. Croix, Lapland, the colony of Georgia, and the Dutch colonies in South America. The Moravians' most conspicuous missionary success in America was among the Delaware Indians (*ibid.,* 28–29; La Rochefoucauld-Liancourt, *Voyage,* VII, 44).

125. The appearance of the sisters does not seem to have elicited much admiration from visitors. "The want of exercise and continual sedentary occupation have given their countenances a deathlike paleness," reported one who visited Bethlehem about the time Dal Verme did. "Their dress, though perfectly neat, does not serve to adorn their persons. Their habit is a short waistcoat which covers the neck, and a petticoat of white linen; their hair is carried back from the forehead, and covered by a linen cap of most unbecoming form; contrived to cover the ears, and tie under the chin; their only ornament is a plain stripe of muslin about two inches wide, surrounding the head, and tied in a small bow behind" (quoted in Martin, *Sketch of Bethlehem,* 41; see also Levering, *Bethlehem,* opp. p. 190).

126. The Sun Inn provided excellent accommodations. John Christian Ebert was landlord of the inn from 1781 to 1790 (Levering, *Bethlehem,* 360–61n.; Lathrop, *Inns and Taverns,* 148–51).

127. In 1769 the farms of the Society were leased to tenants. The overflow stream which ran through the milk house also passed through the place where meat and butter were kept. In 1761, "fine oxen" were seen at Christian's Spring, one of the five Moravian settlements on the Barony of Nazareth. (Levering, *Bethlehem,* 392, 413; George Vaux, ed., "Extract from the Diary of Hannah Callender," *Pa. Mag. of Hist. and Biog.,* XII [1888], 432–56; Shultz and Ettinger, *Nazareth,* 43n.; *Cazenove Journal,* 23–27).

128. David Tannenberg, who built organs for a number of churches in the middle colonies, installed the organ in the Brethren's House in 1776. The single men serenaded the townspeople with hymns on Saturday evenings (Levering, *Bethlehem,* 171–72, 197–203, 363–64, 451).

129. The apothecary shop was completed in 1752 and was in the charge of Dr. John Matthew Otto until his death in 1786. Under the "Economy"

The Middle States and New England 119

the colonists had engaged in group enterprise and received their maintenance from a common store. When this arrangement was terminated the Church retained some real and movable property which it either placed under private operation, as in the case of the tavern and farms, or leased to artisans for the pursuit of their trade (*ibid.*, 256, 378–82, 543–44).

130. See Chastellux, *Travels*, II, 522–23.

131. Other visitors noted the sallowness of complexion resulting from close confinement and lack of exercise (Joshua Gilpin, "Journey to Bethlehem," *Pa. Mag. of Hist. and Biog.*, XLVI [1922], 144). The comments of Luigi Castiglioni, a compatriot of Dal Verme, were similar to those of the latter (*Viaggio*, II, 12). Yet the death records of the Moravian sisters would indicate that the average age of death was not extremely low (the editor is indebted to Vernon Nelson, Archivist, Archives of the Moravian Church, for this information).

132. Every visitor was interested in the water works which were constructed in 1762 by a Danish Moravian resident, Hans Christian Christianson. Six water boxes were situated in the yards of the largest establishments, such as the Sun Inn and the Brethren's and Sisters' houses. The water, which came from a spring, was raised through pipes by means of suction and pressure into a reservoir 80 feet high called the water tower (Martin, *Sketch of Bethlehem*, 20, 28–29; Schoepf, *Travels*, I, 139–40; Levering, *Bethlehem*, 388–92).

133. If, as has been reliably alleged, such reports about the manner of arranging marriages were "canards," they persisted nonetheless. One visitor wrote that the names of the candidates for marriage were placed in two lists and the first of each list proposed as companions for life; if the parties concerned did not approve of the proposed match they could dissent, but in that case they would have no other chance until another list was prepared (Levering, *Bethlehem*, 429n.; Martin, *Sketch of Bethlehem*, 42–43; La Rochefoucauld-Liancourt, *Voyage*, VII, 35–36). For the use of the lot and communal controls over marriage, which gradually declined after the death of Zinzendorf, see Gillian Lindt Gollin, *Moravians in the Two Worlds: A Study of Changing Communities* (New York, 1967), 58, 61–62, 110–27.

134. Nicolaus Ludwig, Count von Zinzendorf (1700–1760) was the restorer and patron, not the founder, of the Unitas Fratrum or Brethren's church, as the Moravian church was also called. This sect had its origin in Bohemia and Moravia in the fifteenth century (Levering, *Bethlehem*, 7–30). The Moravians, as even their critics acknowledged, excelled in agriculture and craftsmanship.

135. Ephrata was established by a schismatic group of Dunkers, the Solitary Brethren of the Community of Seventh Day Baptists, under the leadership of Johann Conrad Beissel (1690–1768), who held that the seventh, not the first, day of the week should be observed as a day of public worship. Beissel came to America from Germany in 1720 and settled at Mill Creek, Pa. He retired to a hermit's cell on the Cocalico Creek in 1725 or 1726, where he was later joined by some of his coreligionists. In 1732 these *Sieben Taeger*, or Seventh Day, Dunkers adopted monasticism. The habit for both sexes, modeled after that worn by the Capuchins, was the same except that the women wore petticoats instead of trousers. The

cenobites took monastic names: Beissel, the spiritual father, was called "Friedsam"; Peter Miller, the prior, "Jaebez"; the sisters chose such romantic names as "Zenobia," "Annastasia," "Iphigenia." La Rochefoucauld-Liancourt, who, like Dal Verme, conversed with Peter Miller, also stated that the monks and nuns took the vows of poverty and chastity, but there is disagreement on this point. Beissel probably favored monasticism (Israel D. Rupp, *History of Lancaster County* [Lancaster, Pa., 1844], 211–34; Franklin Ellis and Samuel Evans, *History of Lancaster County, Pennsylvania, with Biographical Sketches of Many of Its Pioneers and Prominent Men* [Philadelphia, 1883], 838–42; La Rochefoucauld-Liancourt, *Voyage*, I, 61–66; Julius Friedrich Sachse, *The Music of the Ephrata Cloister* [Pennsylvania-German Society Proceedings and Addresses, XII; Lancaster, Pa., 1903], 66–67; Theodore E. Schmauk, *A History of the Lutheran Church in Pennsylvania (1638–1820)* [Lancaster, Pa., 1903], 481–83).

136. Ephrata had a fine and unique musical tradition. Especially impressive were the strange sweetness and beauty of the female voices and the cadences of the combined choirs. The music for the choral singing was set in four, six, and eight parts, with the women taking all but the bass parts. "The performers sat with their heads reclined," wrote an early visitor to Ephrata, "their countenances solemn and dejected, their faces pale and emaciated from their manner of living, the clothing exceedingly white and quite picturesque, and their music such as thrilled to the very soul" (quoted in Rupp, *Lancaster County*, 227; see also Sachse, *Music of Ephrata Cloister*, 9–13; Horace E. Scudder, *Men and Manners in America One Hundred Years Ago* [New York, 1887], 254–56).

137. The earliest hymn and music books used by the Ephrata community were written with pen and ink. Prior to the installation of a printing press, some of their books were printed by Benjamin Franklin. Their hymnal, the *Turtel Taube*, was a quarto volume of 360 pages containing 277 hymns, two-thirds of which were written by Beissel. The Ephrata Baptists also manufactured very fine paper. Probably more than two wagonloads of books were seized during the Revolution. Sheets of paper covered with highly original penmanship and ink painting which decorated the walls of the chapels and dormitories were executed in a scriptorium (Sachse, *Music of Ephrata Cloister*, 13–47; Rupp, *Lancaster County*, 219–22, 226).

138. Sallowness and abdominal swelling are symptoms of tuberculous peritonitis. Beissel set an example for self-mortification, declaring "the Use of Reason in Godly Things void . . . . It cost him and his follower's many Deaths, to remove reason from the Helm" (from Peter Miller's "Introduction [of the tenets of the Rev. Father Conrad Beisel]," p. 2 in "Peter Miller to Benjamin Franklin," June 12, 1771, Franklin Papers B F85X53, American Philosophical Society Library).

139. La Rochefoucauld-Liancourt, who was much more critical of the Ephrata community than Dal Verme, wrote that the monks lived in filth (*Voyage*, I, 66).

140. John Peter Miller (Müller) (1709–96) was probably born at Zweikirchen. He attended the University of Heidelberg and came to Pennsylvania in 1730. Although he was ordained that same year by the

Presbyterians, he found the teachings of the Seventh Day Dunkers more in accord with his own mystical principles. In 1735 he became a Dunker and was rebaptized by Beissel. On the latter's death in 1768, Miller became the head of the Ephrata Community. A man of impressive learning, Miller acted as editor of the works printed at Ephrata and probably was part author of the *Chronicon Ephratense*. He translated the Declaration of Independence into several European languages and was a member of the American Philosophical Society.

141. Evidently the Ephrata cenobites were not absolute vegetarians, as was sometimes reported. All members of the Cloister except the sick were supposed to sleep on boards, but Miller, at least, slept on a feather bed (William F. Worner, *Old Lancaster Tales and Tradition* [Lancaster, Pa., 1927], La Rochefoucauld-Liancourt, *Voyage*, I, 64–65).

142. Lititz, named after a village in Bohemia, was a Moravian community. The Moravian houses for the Brothers and Sisters were not the same as the convents in the Roman Catholic church. The Sisters' house was built in 1758, the Brethren's house a year later (Rupp, *Lancaster County*, 308–24; Mary Augusta Huebener, *A Brief History of Lititz, Pennsylvania* [Lititz, Pa., 1947]).

143. Curtis Grubb (d. 1788) inherited from Peter Grubb the Cornwall furnace and 6,520 acres of land. Robert Coleman acquired by purchase one-sixth of the Cornwall ore-banks; the remaining five-sixths were owned by members of the Grubb family. According to Schoepf, "several short and broken hills running in promiscuous directions are made up almost wholly of good rich ore which lies shallow beneath the surface. To get out this ore nothing whatever need be known of mining" (Ellis and Evans, *Lancaster County*, 301–2; The Pennsylvania Historical and Museum Commission, Harrisburg, "Cornwall Furnace on the Pennsylvania Trail of History"; Schoepf, *Travels*, I, 207–8).

144. Saint Mary's Catholic Church in Lancaster was built in 1762. A bilingual newspaper with alternate columns in German and English, *Die Lancastersche Zeitung/The Lancaster Gazette*, was published biweekly (Frank R. Diffenderfer, *The Story of a Picture* [Lancaster, Pa., 1905], 43–44; Worner, *Lancaster*, 54–55).

145. The Lutheran church was of brick construction. Thomas Anburey described in some detail the interior of the church and the organ which, like the whole of the church, was painted white with gilt decorations. The organ, at that time "reckonized the largest and best in America," was built by David Tannenberg, a German immigrant who lived in Bethlehem and Nazareth before moving to Lititz, Pa. (Worner, *Lancaster*, 46–48; Anburey, *Travels*, II, 303–5).

146. William Henry (1729–86), gunsmith, inventor, patriot, and member of the American Philosophical Society, began his experimental work on the application of steam after his return from a trip to Europe (1761), at which time he met James Watt. Henry has been credited with the invention of the screw auger (Alexander Harris, *A Biographical History of Lancaster County* [Lancaster, Pa., 1872], 278–79; Schoepf, *Travels*, I, 156–57.

147. Gotthilf Henry Ernest Mühlenberg (1753–1815), Lutheran cler-

gyman and botanist. By 1791 Mühlenberg had listed more than 1,100 plants growing in the vicinity of Lancaster.

148. This, the first concert of the season, was held in the Lodge Room. It began at 7 o'clock in the evening. Subscribers' tickets were not transferable; however, officers of the army and navy and "strangers" could obtain single tickets at ten shillings each (*Pennsylvania Journal, and the Weekly Advertiser,* Oct. 8, 1783; *Pennsylvania Packet,* Oct. 9, 1783).

149. Chastellux reported that La Luzerne maintained "a considerable state" and frequently gave large dinners (*Travels,* I, 130–31).

150. William Bartram (1739–1823), author of *The Travels of William Bartram,* was the son of the well-known botanist John Bartram (1699–1777). Schoepf, who visited the Bartram garden at about the same time as Dal Verme, gave this description of it: "In the small space of his garden there are to be found assembled really a great variety of American plants, among others, most of their vines and conifers, species of which very little is generally known." On the other hand, Barbé-Marbois had found the garden "in a state of neglect which caused us actual pain." (Schoepf, *Travels,* I, 90–92; Barbé-Marbois, *Letters,* 131–32; William Bartram, *The Travels of William Bartram,* ed. Francis Harper [New Haven, 1958], xvii–xxxv).

151. Probably the wife of Gen. Walter Stewart, a close friend of Mrs. Washington (Rufus W. Griswold, *The Republican Court; or, American Society in the Days of Washington* [New York, 1864], 337–38; *Appletons' Cyclopaedia of American Biography,* V, 687).

152. The arrival of the Dutch Minister Peter John Van Berckel in Philadelphia "after a tedious and tempestuous passage of 13 weeks from Amsterdam" was greeted by the ringing of bells in Christ Church. Van Berckel, however, was displeased with his reception in Philadelphia (Philadelphia *Independent Gazetteer,* Oct. 18, 1783; *Pennsylvania Gazette,* Oct. 15, 1783; Madison to Edmund Randolph, Oct. 13, 1783, and President of Congress to Peter John Van Berckel, Oct. 25, 1783, Burnett, ed., *Letters,* VII, xxx–xxxi, 333, 355).

153. Peale was careful to portray his subject accurately and was quite proud of his success in this respect. Peale's gallery adjoining his house on the corner of Lombard and Third Streets was a long, narrow construction with skylights. The exhibition hall became known as "Peale's Museum" and "The Philadelphia Museum." It included an assortment of natural curiosities and a miniature "moving-picture" theatre (Charles Coleman Sellers, *The Artist of the Revolution: The Early Life of Charles Willson Peale* [Hebron, Conn., 1939], 16–17, 220, 238, 248–49).

154. For election returns, see *Freeman's Journal: or North-American Intelligencer,* Oct. 22, 1783.

155. Another visitor to Philadelphia, Schoepf, was also skeptical about the success of the porcelain factory. The owner, he said, was a French regimental surgeon and the clay came from Maryland. A chinaware factory in Southwark, perhaps the very one to which the visitors were referring, did prove to be a failure (Schoepf, *Travels,* I, 119; J. Thomas Scharf and Thompson Westcott, *History of Philadelphia, 1609–1884* [Philadelphia, 1884], III, 2297).

156. Chastellux called the little museum of Pierre Eugène du Simitière a cabinet of natural history, with a "rather small and paltry collection." It was advertised as the "American Museum" displaying "natural and artifical curiosities" as well as paintings. The cost of admission was a half dollar (*Travels*, I, 144–45; *Pennsylvania Journal and the Weekly Advertiser*, Sept. 3, 1783; Sellers, *Peale*, 247; Joseph Jackson, *Encyclopedia of Philadelphia* [Harrisburg, 1931–33], III, 914–15).

157. Samuel Vaughan (fl. 1775) or his son, John. The former was a wealthy West Indian merchant, a warm friend of Benjamin Franklin, and an American sympathizer during the Revolution. The Vaughans arrived in Philadelphia on Sept. 8, 1783. During Samuel Vaughan's stay in that city he became a very active member of the American Philosophical Society (Sarah P. Stetson, "The Philadelphia Sojourn of Samuel Vaughan," *Pa. Mag. of Hist. and Biog.*, LXXIII [Oct. 1949], 459–74).

158. The concert was held at the Lodge Room (*Pennsylvania Packet*, Oct. 21, 1783).

159. Janet Wilson, "The Bank of North America and Pennsylvania Politics," *Pa. Mag. of Hist. and Biog.*, LXVI (Jan., 1942), 3–28; F. Cyril James, "The Bank of North America and the Financial History of Philadelphia," *ibid.*, LXIV (Jan., 1940), 56–87; Clarence L. Ver Steeg, *Robert Morris, Revolutionary Financier* (Philadelphia, 1954), 115–17.

160. Presumably the log was kept on the basis of the day starting at the previous noon, instead of midnight, as then was customary.

161. This comparison in parenthesis and the one immediately following it are found in a letter of the same date to Margherita Visconti. This letter has not been reproduced because it is almost identical with the one sent to Count Antonio dal Verme.

Notes to Section 3. The Southern States

1. There were several furnaces in the vicinity of Baltimore. The Kingsbury Furnace and the Lancashire Furnace were the properties of the Principio Company. William Hammond was the manager of the Hocksley Forge on the Patapsco (G. D. Williams, "Mines and Minerals," *Maryland: Its Resources, Industries and Institutions* [Baltimore, 1893], 102–4; Earl Chapin May, *Principio to Wheeling* [New York, 1945], 45–46).
2. Daniel Dulany (1722–97), noted lawyer and Loyalist of Maryland.
3. Probably William Hammond, merchant, or George Hammond (Thomas Waters Griffith, *Annals of Baltimore* [Baltimore, 1824], 103; Robert Purviance, *A Narrative of Events Which Occurred in Baltimore Town during the Revolutionary War* [Baltimore, 1849], 88; Hamilton Owens, *Baltimore on the Chesapeake* [Garden City, N.Y., 1941], 110).
4. Probably Nicholas Rogers, wealthy landowner (Griffith, *Baltimore*, 88; John T. Scharf, *The Chronicles of Baltimore* [Baltimore, 1874], 243; Raphael Semmes, *Baltimore as Seen by Visitors, 1783–1860* [Baltimore, 1953], 12, 23, 27).
5. Possibly Mrs. John Taylor (Scharf, *Chronicles of Baltimore*, 188).
6. Annapolis, of course, not Baltimore, was the capital of Maryland. But Baltimore was becoming a "conceited, bustling and debonair" town at the end of the Revolution (St. George L. Sioussat, "Baltimore, the Monumental City," *Historic Towns of the Southern States*, ed. Lyman P. Powell [New York, 1900], 28).
7. The State House, designed by Joseph Clark, was begun in 1772. Sir Francis Nicholson, who became governor of Maryland in 1694, deserves much credit for having made Annapolis one of the best planned towns in colonial America (Federal Writers' Project, W.P.A., *Maryland, A Guide to the Old Line State* [New York, 1940], 175–82).
8. The question of a permanent capital for the national government received the attention of Congress even before the June events in Philadelphia sent the delegates scurrying to Princeton, which proved to be a most unsatisfactory location for the seat of government. After much sectional argument Congress adopted the following resolutions: (Oct. 7, 1783) "That buildings for the use of Congress be erected on or near the banks of the Delaware, provided a suitable district can be procured . . . , for a federal town; and that the right of soil, and an exclusive or such other jurisdiction as Congress may direct, shall be vested in the United States"; (Oct. 21) "Whereas there is reason to expect that the providing buildings for the alternate residence of Congress in two places will be productive of the most salutary effects, by securing the mutual confidence and affections of the states; *Resolved,* That buildings be likewise erected for the use of Congress, at or near the lower falls of the Potomac or Georgetown; provided a suitable district . . . , can be procured for a federal town

The Southern States *125*

. . . : and that until the buildings to be erected on the banks of the Delaware and Potomac shall be prepared for the reception of Congress, their residence shall be alternately at equal periods, of not more than one year, and not less than six months in Trenton and Annapolis; and the President is hereby authorized and directed to adjourn Congress on the 12th day of November next, to meet at Annapolis on the twenty-sixth day of the same month, for the despatch of public business." Two months later (Dec. 27), a committee appointed to investigate the proposed site at the falls of the Delaware reported that "a preference might be given to the State [Pennsylvania or Delaware] which should secure the soil on the most reasonable terms, and comply with the resolution of Congress respecting the jurisdiction; that the District on the New Jersey side, is at Lamberton, and the District on the Pennsylvania side is near the falls of the Delaware" (*Journals of Continental Congress,* XXV, 657, 714, 841).

9. Perhaps the wife of Thomas Stone (1743–87), signer of the Declaration of Independence.

10. The children were not only naked but also poorly nourished. European travelers never ceased to wonder that naked Negroes and Negresses "should be tumbling about before the party without giving scandal" (Schoepf, *Travels,* II, 47; Janson, *The Stranger in America,* 315–16; Ferdinand M. Bayard, *Travels of a Frenchman in Maryland and Virginia . . . in 1791,* trans. and ed. Ben C. McCary [Williamsburg, Va., 1950], 13).

11. He may have stopped at the old Marlboro House, built *ca.* 1732, and still standing (Federal Writers' Project, *Maryland,* 463–64).

12. Probably George Digges, who represented Prince George Co. in the Maryland House of Delegates (*Maryland Gazette,* Oct. 23, 1783).

13. Thomas Digges (1711–1805) entered the Society of Jesus in 1729. The Diggeses, a distinguished Catholic family of Maryland, lived at Warburton Manor (Peter K. Guilday, *The Life and Times of John Carroll, Archbishop of Baltimore (1735–1815)* [Westminster, Md., 1954], 52–53, 303; Robert H. Elias [pseud. of Thomas Atwood Digges], *Adventures of Alonso,* ed. Thomas J. McMahon [United States Catholic Historical Society, Monograph Series, XVIII; New York, 1943], xiv; Paul Wilstach, *Potomac Landings* [New York, 1921], 107–9; William P. Treacy, *Old Catholic Maryland and Its Early Jesuit Missionaries* [Swedesboro, N.J., n.d.], 133, 179).

14. Thomas Sim Lee (1745–1819), governor of Maryland during and after the Revolution, married Mary Digges (*Genealogical History of the Lee Family of Virginia and Maryland from A.D. 1300 to A.D. 1866,* ed. Edward C. Mead [New York, 1871], 111–13).

15. According to Archbishop Carroll, in 1785 there were nineteen priests in Maryland and five in Pennsylvania. Although the Jesuit order had been abolished, Jesuit priests still owned considerable landed property (Guilday, *John Carroll,* 66; Schoepf, *Travels,* I, 332–33).

16. The Fitzhughs were numerous in the Potomac area. Washington wrote a letter to William Fitzhugh in behalf of Dal Verme. Perhaps the Count was referring to Coronet Peregrine Fitzhugh (Louise Pecquet du Bellet, *Some Prominent Virginia Families* [Lynchburg, Va., 1907], II,

558–76; *Writings of Washington*, ed. Fitzpatrick, XXVII, 165–66; Heitman, *Historical Register*, 176; "The Fitzhughs Family," *Va. Mag. of Hist. and Biog.*, VIII [July, 1900], 91–95).

17. Colonel Robert Townshend Hooe of Alexandria ("History of the Dade Family," *William and Mary Quarterly*, 1st ser., XII [April, 1904], 245–46; *Calendar of Virginia State Papers*, ed. William P. Palmer and Sherwin McRae [Richmond, 1875–93], V, 172; Horace E. Hayden, *Virginia Genealogies* [Washington, D.C., 1931], 716–19).

18. "These falls are 15 miles in length," Jefferson wrote, "and of very great descent, and the navigation above them for batteaux and canoes, is so much interrupted as to be little used" (Jefferson, *Notes*, ed. Peden, 7; see also *The Diaries of George Washington, 1748–1799*, ed. John C. Fitzpatrick [Boston, 1925], II, 403 and n., 424–25).

19. Probably Colonel William Grayson (1736–90), lawyer and Revolutionary soldier, and John Graham (1711–87), merchant. The warehouses at Dumfries were established by act of the Virginia Assembly, Nov. 1769 (Frederick W. Grayson, comp., "The Grayson Family," *Tyler's Quarterly Historical and Genealogical Magazine*, V [Jan. 1924], 197–207; W. B. Chilton, comp., "The Brent Families," *Va. Mag. of Hist. and Biog.*, XIX [Jan. 1911], 95n.; Hayden, *Virginia Genealogies*, 162–63; William W. Hening, comp., *The Statutes at Large; Being a Collection of All the Laws of Virginia* [Richmond, 1823], VIII, 320, XI, 211).

20. General Alexander Spotswood (1751–1818), Revolutionary soldier, was the grandson of Lt. Gov. Alexander Spotswood (Charles Campbell, *Genealogy of the Spotswood Family* [Albany, 1868], 19–20; Andrew G. Grinnan, "Two Spotswood Boys at Eton in 1760, &c.," *William and Mary Quarterly*, 1st ser., II [Oct. 1893], 113–20; Clayton Torrence, "A Cloud-Capped Legion," *ibid.*, 2nd ser., I [Apr. 1921], 137–41).

21. Probably George Webb, Treasurer of Virginia and member of the Council (*Va. Mag. of Hist. and Biog.*, XXV [Jan. 1917], 100; H. R. McIlwain, ed., *Official Letters of the Governors of the State of Virginia* [Richmond, 1926–29], III, 82n.).

22. Probably the Deep Run pits owned by the family of Samuel Du Val. Jefferson wrote that the coal found near Richmond was of excellent quality (*Notes*, ed. Peden, 28; Kathleen Bruce, *Virginia Iron Manufacture in the Slave Era* [New York, 1931], 87–93).

23. The General Assembly of Virginia passed acts for clearing and improving the navigation of the James River in 1765, 1772, and Oct. 1783. The canal was eventually extended to Buchanan in Botetourt County (Hening, *Statutes*, VIII, 148–50, 564–70, XI, 341–42; Bruce, *Iron Manufacture*, 61–62, 88, 92–93).

24. John Banister (1734–88) was the grandson of John Banister, the noted Virginia botanist. During the Revolution he was a colonel in the Virginia Line and served in the Virginia Assembly and the Continental Congress.

25. Probably Henry Walker, county lieutenant for Mecklenburg. In 1783 he was made a trustee for clearing the Roanoke River (*Va. Mag. of Hist. and Biog.*, XXXIV [Apr. 1926], 151; Hening, *Statutes*, XI, 250–52).

The Southern States   127

26. Halifax was the racing capital of North Carolina. Jones was a well-known turfman. The jockeys, Negro boys in the early teens, rode bareback, and there was much betting (John Hervey, *Racing in America, 1665–1865* [New York, 1944], I, 156; William Attmore, "Journal of a Tour to North Carolina," in Hugh T. Lefler, ed., *North Carolina History Told by Contemporaries* [Chapel Hill, N.C., 1934], 131–32).

27. The dance may have been held in the lower floor of the White Hart Lodge, which was planned to serve as a schoolroom, banquet hall, and place of general assembly (Mrs. C. L. Blackburn, "Royal White Hart Lodge," *North Carolina Teacher*, I [Jan., 1925]).

28. Probably Lemuel Hatch, leading citizen of Craven County, N.C. (John Hill Wheeler, *Historical Sketches of North Carolina, from 1584 to 1851* [Philadelphia, 1851], I, 64, 79, 81).

29. Probably Jacob Blount, a prominent public official, merchant, and landowner who lived at Blount Hall in Pitt County. His obituary states that "the distressed, the weary, and the sick traveller, were sure to find a home at Blount-Hall" (*The John Gray Blount Papers*, ed. Alice B. Keith and William H. Masterson [Raleigh, N.C., 1952–65], I, xiv–xvii, 562).

30. Probably Col. John Pugh Williams of Mt. Gallant (James Sprunt, *Chronicles of the Cape Fear River* [Raleigh, N.C., 1916], 71n.).

31. North Carolina law prohibited fire-hunting for the reason given by Dal Verme. Nevertheless this continued to be a most popular sport among the racing and hunting enthusiasts of the southern states. "Sometimes, also," wrote an English visitor, "ludicrous mistakes occurred from the multiplying faculty of the shooter's vision, the amount of game being frequently determined by his amount of brandy" (Bernard, *Retrospections*, 205–6; Walter Clark, ed., *The State Records of North Carolina* [Goldsboro, N.C., 1886–1907], XXIII, 955–56).

32. John Alexander Lillington (*ca.* 1725–1867), a Barbadian by birth, attained the rank of brigadier general during the Revolution (*Cyclopaedia of American Biography*, III, 712; Sprunt, *Chronicles of Cape Fear*, 69, 71).

33. Probably John Swann of Swann's Point (Sprunt, *Chronicles of Cape Fear*, 71n.; Wheeler, *Historical Sketches*, I, 47).

34. Archibald McLaine, patriot and prominent member of the Wilmington bar (Wheeler, *Historical Sketches*, II, 290; Sprunt, *Chronicles of Cape Fear*, 76, 92, 110–11, 565; John W. Moore, *History of North Carolina* [Raleigh, N.C., 1880], I, 383).

35. Dal Verme was not alone in complaining about the terrible roads, the extravagant prices, and the lack of accommodations in North Carolina. The keeper of a private guest house did not have to pay the tax collected for dispensing liquor, hence the number of such houses (Bernard, *Retrospections*, 202–5; Janson, *The Stranger in America*, 315–17; Schoepf, *Travels*, II, 35–36; Hunter, *Quebec to Carolina*, 281–84).

36. Probably the same tavern where Washington lodged on April 27, 1791 (Archibald Henderson, *Washington's Southern Tour, 1791* [Boston, 1923], 125).

37. This was probably the Long Bay or Beach Road described by Schoepf. "Here for 16 miles the common highway runs very near the shore. Lonely and desolate as this part of the road is, without shade and with no

dwellings in sight, it is by no means a tedious road" (*Travels*, II, 161–62).

38. Col. William Alston, Revolutionary soldier and wealthy planter. Washington stayed overnight at the Alston mansion, Clifton House, when he visited South Carolina in 1791 (Henderson, *Washington's Southern Tour*, 126–27).

39. Probably Col. Robert Heriot; or George Heriot or William Heriot, Treasurer of the Winyaw Indigo Society (Alexander S. Salley, ed., *Stub Entries to Indents Issued in Payment against South Carolina Growing out of the Revolution*, Book B [Columbia, S.C., 1934], 161; *ibid.*, Books R-T [Columbia, S.C., 1917], 145; *ibid.*, Books Y-Z [Columbia, S.C., 1927], 298; Mabel L. Webber, comp., "Marriage and Death Notices from the Charleston Morning Post; and Daily Advertiser, and Its Successor the City Gazette," *S.C. Hist. and Geneal. Mag.*, XXI [July, 1920], 125; *ibid.*, XXXII [July, 1931], 197–98).

40. Foreign visitors to South Carolina were very much interested in the processing of indigo. Castiglioni reported that the rice yield per acre was less in South Carolina than in Lombardy, but that the Carolina rice was fatter and whiter (*Viaggio*, I, 322–26; Schoepf, *Travels*, II, 157–60; Janson, *Stranger in America*, 376–78; La Rochefoucauld-Liancourt, *Voyage*, IV, 139–41).

41. Thomas Ferguson, wealthy South Carolinian and intimate friend of Christopher Gadsden. The two were among the seventy-eight citizens of Charleston imprisoned by the British at St. Augustine in 1780 (Harriette K. Leiding, *Historic Houses of South Carolina* [Philadelphia, 1921], 54–57; Joseph Johnson, *Traditions and Reminiscences Chiefly of the American Revolution in the South* [Charleston, S.C., 1851], 367).

42. Probably Edward Rutledge (1749–1800), signer of the Declaration of Independence, governor of South Carolina, and wealthy planter. His brother, John Rutledge (1739–1800), statesman, jurist, and governor of South Carolina during the darkest period in the Revolutionary history of that state, was elected to Congress in 1783. He returned to Charleston on the *Patsey Rutledge*, Dec. 11, 1783 (*South Carolina Gazette and General Advertiser*, Dec. 9–13, 1783).

43. Probably Thomas Farr (d. 1788), whose estate was called Hickory Hill (Henry A. M. Smith, "The Ashley River: Its Seats and Settlements," *S.C. Hist. and Geneal. Mag.*, XX [Apr., 1919], 84–85, 135n.).

44. Thomas Bee, South Carolina statesman and judge (*Appleton's Cyclopaedia of American Biography*, I, 216).

45. Probably George Abbott Hall, Revolutionary patriot imprisoned at St. Augustine following the British capture of Charleston in May 1780. President Washington appointed Hall collector of the port of Charleston (Johnson, *Traditions and Reminiscences*, 130, 198, 332).

46. Possibly William Blake (1739–1803) (*S.C. Hist. and Geneal. Mag.*, I [Apr., 1900], 161–62).

47. Andrew Turnbull (1718–92), physician and founder of the ill-fated colony of New Smyrna in Florida settled by Mediterranean immigrants. His wife was Maria Gracia Dura Bin, a Greek of Smyrna. The Turnbulls settled in Charleston in 1781.

48. Possibly Thomas Farrar or Field Farrar (*ibid.,* VII [Oct., 1906], 219).

49. Schoepf reported that there were as many as twenty different social clubs in Charleston and that many people belonged to more than one of them. These organizations bore strange names: Mount Sion Society, Hellfire Club, Marine Anti-Brittanic Society, Smoking Society. The following one was among the regulations of the Saint George's Club:

> To be furnish'd on each Club day a Barb^d
> Lamb or Shoat as the season may suit
> 1 Round of Beef or Beef Stakes
> 1 Ham, 1 Turkey, 6 Fowls
> 1 Loaf sugar, Bread, Rice
> 1 doz Wine, 3 Gall^s. Rum, 100 Times
> ½ Gall^n Brandy
> Pipes & Tobacco or 100 Segars.

The membership and rules for the Jockey Club and Saint George's Club are given in *S.C. Hist. Geneal. Mag.,* VIII (Apr. 1907), 88–94. See also Schoepf, *Travels,* II, 168–69.

50. Perhaps Dal Verme meant Coffee House (Henderson, *Washington's Southern Tour,* 160n.).

51. Ralph Izard (1741/2–1804), Revolutionary patriot, diplomat, and statesman, had very extensive holdings in South Carolina devoted to the cultivation of rice and indigo. Izard was cosmopolitan in his interests and tastes, having lived in London and Paris and made the grand tour of Europe with a long pause in Rome. In 1777 Congress elected him Commissioner to Tuscany, but he was never received by that government.

52. Thanksgiving services were held on Thursday, Dec. 11, at St. Philip's, St. Michael's, and the Independent Church where public worship had not been held since May 1780 (*S.C. Gazette and General Advertiser,* Dec. 9–13, 1783).

53. Maj. Edmund M. Hyrne, a member of the General Assembly, died at the age of 35 from a head wound he had received in 1780. During the Revolution he served as aide-de-camp to Gen. Nathanael Greene and was cited by Congress for his conduct at the Battle of Eutaw Springs in 1781. As Commissary of Prisoners he negotiated the exchange of prisoners which freed the Charlestonians confined at St. Augustine. Hyrne's funeral, attended by all the dignitaries of the South Carolina capital, was held in St. Michael's Church (*ibid.*).

54. The Colonial Exchange was built in 1771. During the Revolution it was used as a prison and as a secret magazine (Yates Snowden "Charleston," in Powell, ed., *Historic Towns of the Southern States,* 286).

55. Lawrence Furlong, *The American Coast Pilot* (Newburyport, Mass., 1804), 194–95 and map; *The English Pilot. The Fourth Book* (London, 1780).

Notes to Section 5. The West Indies

1. George Smith and John Smith were merchants of Antigua (Vere Langford Oliver, *The History of the Island of Antigua* [London, 1892–99], III, 94–99).
2. Very likely Smith's Tavern where travelers generally stopped (John Luffman, *A Brief Account of the Island of Antigua . . . in Letters to a Friend, Written in the Years 1786, 1787, 1788* [London, 1790], 101).
3. Thomas Shirley, son of Governor William Shirley, was appointed governor of the Leeward Islands in 1781. The seat of the governor was at Clark's Hill, about five miles from St. John's (Maria W. Riddell, *Voyages to the Madeira, and Leeward Caribbean Isles* [Edinburgh, 1792], 49).
4. Probably "Mr. Druce, the agent victualer" mentioned in a letter written by Horatio Nelson, Aug. 3, 1784, when he was in Antigua ([N. A.], *Antigua and the Antiguans: A Full Account of the Colony and Its Inhabitants* [2 vols., London, 1844], I, 269n.).
5. Probably Alexander Scott, a merchant of Antigua, who died Jan. 13, 1789 (*Caribbeana*, ed. Vere Langford Oliver, V [Oct., 1918], pt. 8, 308–9).
6. This dinner was probably held in the Courthouse, which was one of the finest buildings in the British West Indies; public dinners and balls were held there (Luffman, *Antigua*, 21–22; Oliver, *Antigua*, cxxv).
7. The Council of Antigua was composed of twelve members and the Assembly of twenty-five members. The governor of the Leeward Islands generally resided at Antigua (Bryan Edwards, *The History, Civil and Commercial, of the British West Indies* [5 vols., London, 1819], II, 486–87; Elsa V. Goveia, *Slave Society in the British Leeward Islands at the End of the Eighteenth Century* [New Haven, 1965], 51–55).
8. This destructive fire occurred on April 10, 1782. The use of shingles instead of tiles for roofing was largely responsible for the conflagration. The Friendly Fire Company was organized after the fire, and building regulations were passed requiring the use of stone or brick and the casing of roofs with tiles or slates (Luffman, *Antigua*, 23–24; *Antigua and Antiguans*, 117–18).
9. Probably John Burke, a prominent lawyer, appointed solicitor general of the Leeward Islands April 9, 1785, and elected speaker Aug. 12, 1785 (Oliver, *Antigua*, I, 84–87, cxxviii; Luffman, *Antigua*, 39–40).
10. Probably John Rose, merchant and provost marshal of Antigua (Oliver, *Antigua*, III, 52–54; *Caribbeana*, V [Oct. 1918], pt. 8, 308).
11. The market, a noisy and malodorous affair, was held at the southern extremity of the town. It began at daybreak and ended in midafternoon (Luffman, *Antigua*, 94–95, 138–41).
12. The church, dedicated to St. John, was built of bricks and stone. The

organ was constructed in 1760 at a cost of £450 sterling (*ibid.*, 21; *Antigua and Antiguans*, 219–34).

13. Probably Cornelius Sherman of Parham. The village of Parham, five miles east of St. John's, had only one principal street; although it had a good harbor and a custom house, it had little commerce (Luffman, *Antigua*, 26; Oliver, *Antigua*, II, 171).

14. Probably Ann Ronan (b. 1765) and Margaret Ronan (b. 1759), daughters of Philip Ronan. Guana Isle, formerly called Guiana Island for the English settlers who emigrated from Guiana, is a small island off the coast of Antigua (Oliver, *Antigua*, III, 50–51; *Antigua and Antiguans*, 159).

15. Antigua suffered from a succession of droughts, especially in 1779 and 1789, which impoverished many affluent families. In 1783 the Council and Assembly of Antigua petitioned Parliament to declare St. John's and Parham free ports. Economic necessity was perhaps responsible for the great number of landowners who were permanent residents of the island (Robson Lowe, *The Codrington Correspondence, 1743–1851* [London, 1951], 22; Edwards, *West Indies*, II, 521–22; Oliver, *Antigua*, I, cxxvii; Lowell J. Ragatz, *The Fall of the Planter Class in the British Caribbean, 1763–1833* [New York, 1928], 66–67).

16. In 1786 the population of Antigua was estimated at 50,000, of whom only 5,000 were whites. In 1791 Bryan Edwards reported a population of 2,590 whites and 37,808 Negroes. The census of 1787 gave Antigua 2,590 whites; 1,230 free Negroes; 37,808 slaves (Luffman, *Antigua*, 15–16; Edwards, *West Indies*, II, 2; Sir William Young, *The West-India Common-Place Book* [London, 1807], 3).

17. The food allowance also included beans, rice, salt beef or pork, and plantain. The common breakfast for Negroes consisted of boiled yams, eddoes, okra, calalue, and plantains seasoned with salt and cayenne pepper; for dinner they also had salted or pickled fish. When a Negro reached the age of 14 or 15 he was given a small garden 25 to 30 feet square (Luffman, *Antigua*, 94–95; Edwards, *West Indies*, II, 158–59).

18. Janet Schaw, who visited Antigua in 1774, reported no instances of cruelty. Indeed, on one large plantation she noted that the slaves were so "well fed" and "well supported" that they appeared to be "the subjects of a good prince." Bryan Edwards declared that "although . . . enormities have certainly *sometimes* happened, . . . the *general* treatment of the Negroes in the British West Indies is mild, temperate, and indulgent." On the other hand, Luffman wrote: "Many slaves, who cannot properly be said to be murdered, die from want of care, or continual ill-usage, which the law . . . cannot take cognizance of." Slaves who violated a curfew at 9:45 in the evening were flogged (Janet Schaw, *Journal of a Lady of Quality*, ed. Evangeline W. and Charles M. Andrews [New Haven, 1923], 104; Edwards, *West Indies*, II, 169–70; Luffman, *Antigua*, 102–8, 126, 130–34; Goveia, *Slave Society*, 152–202).

19. St. John's was about three-quarters of a mile long and a half mile wide. The houses were generally built of wood and were low in height on account of the incidence of hurricanes and earthquakes. The streets were

not only unpaved but also dirty (Luffman, *Antigua*, 20–21; Oliver, *Antigua*, I, cxxv).

20. In addition to frequent earthquakes and the disastrous fire of 1782, Antigua suffered other calamities—droughts, hurricanes, epidemics, and insurrections. For a list of these, see Lowe, *Codrington Correspondence*, 6, 22.

21. Baron de Clugny was appointed governor of Guadeloupe July 20, 1783. Since he did not arrive in the colony until May 27, 1784, Beaumé de Saulais acted as governor. François de Foulquier was the intendant (Alfred A. Martineau and L.-Ph. May, *Trois Siècles D'Histoire Antillaise Martinique et Guadeloupe* [Paris, 1935], 87, 200, 250).

22. This elite corps, officially recognized by the king and exempt from the corvée and from guard and patrol duty in peacetime, went on maneuvers twice a year, in January and July. Once a year they engaged in fire exercise (C. A. Banbuck, *Histoire Politique, Économique et Sociale de la Martinique Sous l'Ancien Régime* (1635–1789) [Paris, 1935], 146).

23. The Capuchin church was in the "Quartier des Habitans" (Eugène-Édouard Boyer-Peyreleau, *Les Antilles Françaises, Particulièrement La Guadeloupe* [2 vols., Paris, 1823], I, 199).

24. For a summary of the juridical position of Negroes, both slave and free, see Maurice Satineau, *Histoire De La Guadeloupe Sous l'Ancien Régime* (Paris, 1918), 270–360.

25. Fort Saint-Charles, renamed Fort Richepanse in 1803, was poorly situated and virtually indefensible against attack from outlying heights. Instead of replacing the fort in a better location it was strengthened in 1766 by the addition of bastions, redoubts, and other military constructions (Boyer-Peyreleau, *Les Antilles*, I, 184–86).

26. The cassava, or manioc, plant was the source of cassava flour and bread. This nutritious food was obtained by pressing the poisonous juice from the plant and then drying or baking the remaining part, which was eaten dry or toasted and was also used for making puddings (Luffman, *Antigua*, 63; M. Félix Renouard, [Marquis] de Sainte-Croix, *Statistique De La Martinique* [2 vols., Paris, 1822], II, 106).

27. So widespread was contraband trade in the French West Indies that special regulations to check it were issued in 1784 (Banbuck, *Martinique*, 330–35).

28. The loss caused by this disastrous fire which occurred on Aug. 15, 1782, was estimated at 2,200,000 livres (Boyer-Peyreleau, *Les Antilles*, I, 179).

29. The French under the command of Marquis de Bouillé, governor of Martinique, took Dominica in Sept. 1778, and held it until Jan. 1783, at which time it was restored to Great Britain. On the evening of Easter Sunday 1781, a disastrous fire consumed about five hundred houses and a large quantity of merchandise. The English residents charged the French with making little or no effort to save English property from the flames. After the Revolution, Roseau was again declared a free port by act of Parliament (Edwards, *West Indies*, I, 434–42; Thomas Coke, *A History of the West Indies* [3 vols., Liverpool, 1808–11], II, 340–41; Young, *Common-Place Book*, 174–75).

The West Indies 133

30. The chief seat of government in Martinique was at Fort-Royal. Saint-Pierre was the commercial center (C. C. Robin, *Voyages dans L'Intérieur de la Louisiane, de la Floride Occidentale, et dans les Isles de la Martinique et de Saint-Domingue* . . . *1802, 1803, 1804, 1805, 1806* [Paris, 1807], I, 49; M. Adrien Dessales, *Histoire générale des Antilles* [Paris, 1847–48], 282, 350; Martineau and May, *Trois Siècles d'Histoire Antillaise*, 132; Jacques Peuchet, *État des Colonies et du Commerce* [2 vols., Paris, 1821], II, 577–78).

31. This was probably "L'Église du Fort" (Renouard, *Statistique de la Martinique*, II, 80).

32. The Sunday fairs held in Saint-Pierre, Fort-Royal (Fort-de-France), and Trinité displayed dry goods, hardware, jewelry, and other articles. On this day and on special feast days between masses the Negroes were permitted to sell their surplus produce, including fruit and fowl, at the market. The money they received was used to purchase fish, meat, and rice to supplement their normal diet of vegetables. Sunday being a free day, they could cultivate their own garden or hire themselves out at the rate of two francs for the day (Satineau, *Guadeloupe*, 263–64; Robin, *Voyages*, I, 71).

33. The theatre was in the Paroisse Du Fort (Renouard, *Statistique de la Martinique*, II, 79).

34. The three favorite dances of the Negroes were called the "Calenda," a dance "trés lascive et trés fatigante," the "Vaudoux," and the "Don Pèdre." In the towns slaves imitated the dances of their masters. The passionate intensity of their dancing, in which the movements of the legs were subordinated to those of the body and face, greatly impressed European observers (Robin, *Voyages*, I, 42–43; Satineau, *Guadeloupe*, 274–77; Dessales, *Histoire des Antilles*, III, 297).

35. The sugar loaf or turban effect of the Negresses' headdress, known as the "Tenah," was obtained by tying around the head as many as ten or twelve handkerchiefs. This fashion, however, was largely confined to the more opulent, lighter-hued urban dwellers (Schaw, *Journal*, 108n.; Satineau, *Guadeloupe*, 272).

36. In all of the West Indies, Negro children went about naked and adult slaves of both sexes wore very little clothing. There were exceptions, of course, especially among the free Negroes and mulattoes (Satineau, *Guadeloupe*, 270–71; Schaw, *Journal*, 87, 107–8).

37. The journey from Saint-Pierre to Fort-Royal was usually made by water since the land route was difficult and hilly (Renouard, *Statistique de la Martinique*, II, 5).

38. The Vicomte de Damas de Marillac became acting governor of Martinique in 1782 and governor in May 1784. De Peinier was the intendant at the time of Dal Verme's visit. Fort Bourbon, which dominated Fort-Royal, was dismantled by the English in 1809 (*ibid.*, I, 137, 142, 144, II, 3).

39. According to Necker's statistics of 1779, Martinique had a population of 85,000, of whom 71,000 were slaves. Moreau de Saint-Méry, in 1790, put the number of slaves in Martinique at 76,000. Guadeloupe's population was larger. Mills were indispensable at the sugar refineries.

Before the introduction of steam mills, watermills were preferred to those powered by animals. Windmills were the least dependable (Serge Denis, *Nos Antilles Trois siècles de vie française* [Paris, 1935], 69, 74; Boyer-Peyreleau, *Les Antilles Françaises*, I, 281–83).

40. Bordeaux was the principal French port engaged in colonial trade (Renouard, *Statistique de la Martinique*, II, 267).

41. This island was also spelled Zancheo and Zachea (*The English Pilot. The Fourth book* [1780]; *ibid.* [1775], 33). Dal Verme called the island *Les Achés*.

42. Guillaume Léonard de Bellecombe served as governor of Santo Domingo from Feb. 14, 1782, to July 3, 1785. Jacques Alexandre de Bongars served for the second time as intendant from Feb. 14, 1782, to Nov. 9, 1785 (Moreau de Saint-Méry, *Description De La Partie Française De L'Isle Saint-Domingue*, ed. Blanche Maurel and Étienne Taillemite [Paris, 1958], I, 18–19).

43. Ten loges in the back of the theatre were reserved for mulattoes and Negroes (*ibid.*, I, 385).

44. The Government House, which the Jesuits had occupied from 1748 to 1763, was quite spacious. For a detailed description, see *ibid.*, I, 370–71, 384–87.

45. Possibly François Jean Baptiste Gautier de la Rivière or Pierre Gautier (*ibid.*, I, 145, III, 1493).

46. François Louis Joseph de Laborde de Marcheville perished in a shipwreck while on an expedition to circumnavigate the earth. A brother also lost his life in this disaster. The father, Jean Joseph, Marquis de Laborde, was court banker under Louis XV and Louis XVI and was guillotined in 1794 (*ibid.*, II, 629n., III, 1504).

47. Henry Pantaléon, Comte de Macnémara, naval officer and Chevalier of the Order of St. Louis (1775), was assassinated at L'Ile de France, Sept. 4, 1790 (*ibid.*, III, 1520).

48. The Church of Notre Dame was 206 feet long and 84 feet wide (*ibid.*, I, 335).

49. The French king's letter of Nov. 17, 1783, to Gov.-Gen. Bellecombe gave specific instructions regarding the peace celebration: "mon intention est que vous fassiez chanter le *Te Deum* dans la principale Église du Port-au-Prince, et dans les autres Églises de la Colonie, et que vous y assistiez dans le lieu de votre résidence, et fassiez assister le Conseil-Supérieur, que vous teniez la main à ce que les autres Corps qui doivent être à de semblables Cérémonies, ayent a s'y trouver, et qu'au surplus, vous donniez les Ordres nécessaires dans la Colonie pour faire allumer des feux-de-joie dans le rues, tirer le cannon, et donner toutes les autres marques et démonstrations de réjouissances publiques accoutumées en pareil cas" (Moreau de Saint-Méry, *Loix Et Constitutions Des Colonies Françoises De L'Amérique Sous Le Vent* [6 vols., Paris, 1784–90], VI, 396–97).

50. Probably Antoine Jean Baptiste Paulin Walsh, wealthy planter (Moreau de Saint-Méry, *Saint-Domingue*, III, 1559).

51. Probably Stephen Ceronio, agent for the United States at Cap-Français (*The Revolutionary Diplomatic Correspondence of the United States,*

ed. Francis Wharton [Washington, D.C., 1889], II, 181–82; *Journals of Congress*, VIII, 217–18, XX, 515).

52. For a description and plan of Cap-Français, see Moreau de Saint-Méry, *Saint-Domingue*, 294 ff.; "Plan De La Ville Du Cap François et Ses Environs," *ibid.*, endpaper.

53. There was, however, a considerable increase in the number of houses in Martha Brae and in the volume of shipping in the port of Falmouth during the period 1770–90 (Edwards, *West Indies*, I, 263–64; William Beckford, *A Descriptive Account of the Island of Jamaica* [2 vols., London, 1790], I, xxvi, xxviii).

54. Quakers visited Jamaica shortly after its capture by the English in 1655. Dal Verme's hospitable friend was probably Isaac L. Winn, a successful sugar producer and director of the Close Harbour Company and the Falmouth Water Company. The inhabitants of Jamaica, where travelers were few and taverns scarce, were noted for their liberal hospitality (Rufus M. Jones, *The Quakers in the American Colonies* [London, 1911], 43; Ragatz, *The Fall of the Planter Class*, 64; Robert Renny, *An History of Jamaica with Observations* [London, 1807], 324; Beckford, *Jamaica*, I, 267–68; for help in identifying names of Jamaicans the editor is indebted to Miss Rema Falconer of the Institute of Jamaica).

55. Horseback was the usual mode of travel over the steep, rough, and narrow roads of the mountain districts (Renny, *Jamaica*, 324).

56. Perhaps Edward Clarke or his father George Hyde Clarke, who inherited extensive real and personal property in Jamaica (*Caribbeana*, ed. Oliver, I [Oct., 1910], pt. 8, 375).

57. Rio Bueno divided Trelawney Parish from St. Ann's (Thomas Coke, *A History of the West Indies* [3 vols., Liverpool, 1808–11], I, 348, 365).

58. Dry Harbour is in St. Ann's Parish, North Jamaica. Nearby are caves with aboriginal remains (James M. Philippo, *Jamaica: Its Past and Present State* [Philadelphia, 1843], 23).

59. Thomas Coke also noted in this part of Jamaica "an abundance of very fine pasturage and a great quantity of cattle." The precipices of Mount Diablo, a peak of 2,750 ft., "far exceeded" his expectations "in the awfulness and horror of their appearance" (*Extracts of the Journals of the Late Rev. Thomas Coke, L.L.D.* [Dublin, 1816], 154–55; Coke, *West Indies*, I, 419).

60. The population of Spanish Town was probably less than 3,000. The King's House, where the governor resided, was completed in 1762 at a cost of £21,428 sterling. This fine two-storied brick building, regarded as one of the most elegant in British America, faced a square on the opposite side of which stood other public buildings. Maj. Gen. Archibald Campbell was succeeded as governor in 1784 by Brig. Gen. Alured Clark (J. B. Moreton, *Manners and Customs in the West India Islands* [London, 1790], 36–37; *Lady Nugents' Journal: Jamaica One Hundred Years Ago*, ed. Frank Cundall [London, 1907], 14, 17; Edwards, *West Indies*, I, 260; W. Alexander Feurtado, *Official and Other Personages of Jamaica from 1655 to 1790* [Kingston, 1896], XI.

61. Hugh O'Connor was lieutenant of the Kingston militia, 1794. Charles O'Connor was lieutenant of the Trelawney militia, 1794, and assistant judge, Court of Common Pleas.

62. The distance between Spanish Town and Kingston was thirteen miles. For a list of post roads throughout Jamaica *ca.* 1790, as well as distances between various points on the island, see Beckford, *Descriptive Account of Jamaica,* I, xxxvii. See also Frederick G. Spurdle, *Early West Indian Government* (Palmerston North, N.Z., 1963), 141–42.

63. Probably Richard Lake, judicial official and civic leader of Kingston.

64. Probably Archibald Thomson, merchant of Kingston and member of the Assembly (Feurtado, *Personages of Jamaica,* 94).

65. Other travelers commented on the very poor church attendance. "It is a pity that the morals of the people are not corrected," Moreton wrote, "so as to have it as much frequented by the living as the dead." Mulattoes attended more faithfully and in greater number than the whites (*Manners and Customs,* 34; see also Renny, *Jamaica,* 326–27).

66. Probably James Pinnock, clerk of the Supreme Court (1774), counselor (1780), and member of the Assembly from St. Thomas Parish (Feurtado, *Personages of Jamaica,* 77).

67. The famous English corsair was John Porkins, commander of the *Endeavor*. In July 1783, four Frenchmen were condemned to death for having corresponded with this formidable enemy (Moreau de Saint-Méry, *Loix et Constitutions,* VI, 129, 301–2, 333–34; *Saint-Domingue,* III, 1389).

68. Sieurs Vincendon received permission, Oct. 2, 1783, to publish a "Journal Américain, ou Relations Historiques, Politiques, Littéraires, de Jurisprudence, de Commerce et d'Agriculture," on condition that it not be printed, sold, or distributed until its contents had been approved by the highest executive and judicial officials of Santo Domingo (Moreau de Saint-Méry, *Loix et Constitutions,* VI, 349–50).

INDEX

Index

Acadians, 27, 115
Accademia dei Trasformati, xiv
Adams, John, xi, 39, 97
Adams, Samuel, 20
Albany, N.Y., 12, 106
Albert, *see* Litta, Alberto
Alexandria, Va., 47, 49
Alston, William, xxxii, 53, 127
America, ship, 23
American encampment, 11, 106
American Society, 43
Amphion, ship, 71
Annapolis, Md., 46-47, 124
Antigua, 64, 66, 130, 131-32
Appomattox River, 50
Ariosto, xiii
Assembly House, Portsmouth, N.H., 112
Atyataghronghta, Col. Louis, 13, 106-7
Avall, Mr., 73

Balls, *see* Dancing
Baltimore, Md., 46, 124
Banister, Col. John, xxxii, 50, 126
Bank of North America, 37
Barbé-Marbois, François, Marquis de, xxxi
Barbeque, 55
Barela, Sigr., 83
Barrington, Mass., 19
Bartram, William, xxx, 35, 122
Bartram garden, 35, 102, 122
Basse-Terre, 66, 68, 69
Beauregard, Abbé, 76
Beccaria, Marquis Cesare, xix
Bee, Thomas, xxxii, 54, 55, 56
Beeckman, Johannes Jacobse, 106
Beissel, Conrad, 33, 119-20
Bel Air, Md., 46
Belgioioso, Count Lodovico, xii, 97
Bellano, falls, 10, 105

Belle Alise, ship, 70
Belloni, Sigr., 83
Belvidere, N.J., 30-31
Beresford, Richard, 28
Bethlehem, Pa., 31-32, 118-19; *see also* Moravians
Bidley, Mr., 75
Birch, Brig. Gen. Samuel, 7
Bird houses, 20
Birds, xxix
Black, Mr., *see* Blake, William
Blake, William, 54, 55
Bland, Theodorick, 10, 30
Bland, Mrs. Theodorick, 30, 36
Blount, Col. Jacob, 51, 127
Bokley, Mr., *see* Gokley
Boston, Mass., xxxi, 20-21, 24
Boudinot, Elias, 10, 20, 37, 39, 106
Bouillé, Marquis de, 132
Bowdoin, James, xxxii, 20, 23, 92, 97
Bowen, Jabez, 25
Bowers, 14, 17, 108
Brant, Joseph, 110
Breck, Samuel, 24, 25, 92, 114
Brenton, Benjamin, 26
Bridges: in Middle States and New England, 15, 16, 19, 21; in Southern States, 52
Brookfield, Mass., 19
Brown, Moses, 26
Brown, Sarah, 26, 114
Buccleuch, Henry, Duke of, xxii
Bunker Hill, Mass., xxxi, 20
Burgoyne, John, xxii, 13
Burke, John, 64
Butler, Capt. Walter, 110

Caccia, banker, xi
Cadiz, 81, 83, 85
Cambridge, Mass., 23, 24, 25
Campbell, Maj. Gen. Archibald, 135

Campbell, Samuel, 110
Canajoharie, 17, 110, 111
Canals, 17, 50, 126
Cape Fear River, 51
Cap-Français, 71, 73, 76, 134
Capital, U.S., 124-25
Carleton, Sir Guy, 44
Carriages, xxix, 10, 23, 83, 86, 104-5
Cary, Archibald, 98
Casamajor, Mr., 68
Cassava flour, 68, 132
Castiglione, Marquise, xxii
Castiglione, Mme. de, 100
Castiglioni, Count Luigi, *Viaggio Negli Stati Uniti dell' America Settentrionale*, xvii, xxvi, xxvii, 92, 93, 98-99, 100, 101
Castle, Boston, 112
Celebrations: anniversary of Independence, 10; of peace, 55, 71-72, 134; of St. Louis, 113
Celsi, Doge Lorenzo, xiii
Ceronio, Stephen, 72
Certosa, Abbey, xix
Chace, Samuel, 26
Champlin, Christopher, xxxii, 26, 114
Charles VIII of France, xiv
Charles River, 21
Charleston, S.C., xxxi, 54, 56, 58; society, 102
Charlestown, Mass., 20-21, 112
Charlestown, R.I., 26
Cherry Valley, 17, 110
Chester, Pa., 36, 46
Christiana Bridge, Del., 46
Church (Carter), Mrs. Angelica Schuyler, 13, 106
Churches, *see* Houses of worship
Cisalpine Republic, xvi
Clark, Brig. Gen. Alured, 135
Clark, Edward, 74-75
Clark, Joseph, 124
Clinton, George, 12, 109, 111
Clubs, 23, 54, 56, 129, 130
Clugny, Baron de, 132
Cohoes Falls, xxix, 107
Coke, Rev. Thomas, 135-36

Colchester, Va., 49
Coleman, Robert, 34
Collect Pond, 8
College of New Jersey, 10, 30, 39, 117
College of Rhode Island, 25, 114
Commencements, *see* Colleges
Commerce, 43, 86
Conanicut Island, 26
Concerts, 35, 37, 55, 58, 122
Conforno, Sigr., 60
Congress, 7
Connecticut River, 19, 27
Conner, "Tom," 109
Contraband, 69, 132
Cooper, Dr. Samuel, 20
Corn on cob, 21
Cornstalk, murder of, xxix
Corunna, 81, 85
Cosway, Maria, xviii
Creoles, 68
Crown Point, 14, 108
Cushing, Thomas, xxxii, 20, 24
Cushing, William, xxxii, 24

Damas de Marillac, Vicomte de, 133
Dancing, 22, 24, 26, 27, 30, 50, 54, 55, 58, 72, 114, 127
D'Aquino, Giacomo, Prince Caramanico, xi, xii, 97
Darell, Capt., 56
Deblois, Miss, 23, 113
Deblois, Mrs. William, 23
Delaware River, 28, 31
Dickinson, John, xxxii, 35
Digges, George, xxxii, 47
Digges, Rev. Thomas, xxxii, 47
Dominica, 69, 132
Druce, Mr., 63
Dry Harbour, 75, 135
Dulaney, Daniel, 46
Dumfries, Va., 49
Dunkers, 33-34, 119-21
Dupuis, Capt., 70
Dwight, Timothy, 115
Dyant, Mr., 69

Earthquakes, 66, 132
Easton, Pa., 30

Elections in Pa., 36
Elizabeth, N.J., 8, 10-11, 28
Endeavor, ship, 136
Ephrata, Pa., xxxii, 33-34; see also Dunkers
Exchange, Charleston, S.C., 129

Factories, 36, 122
Fairs, see Markets
Falmouth, Jamaica, 135
Farr, Thomas, 54, 55, 128
Farrar, Thomas, 54
Fate, Mr., 75
Ferguson, Thomas, 54, 128
Fire clubs, see Clubs
Fires, 23, 64, 69, 103-4, 130, 131, 132
Fireworks, 72, 105
Firmian, Count Karl Joseph, xv, xx-xxi
Fish, 14
Fitzgerald, John, 98
Fitzhugh, Capt., 47
Fitzhugh, Col., 49
Fitzhugh, William, 98, 125
Fitzhughs, xxxii
Flying squirrel, xxix, 30-31, 117
Fog, antidotes for, 15
Fontane, Mr., 70
Fort-Royal, 69-70, 133
Forts: frontier, 108; at Portsmouth, N.H., 112; Fort Aldemar, see Fort Herkimer; Fort Bourbon, 70, 133; Fort Crown Point, 14; Fort Dayton, 16, 110; Fort Edward, 13-14, 15, 108; Fort Etham, see Fort Dayton; Fort George, 13, 103, 108; Fort Griswold, 26, 115; Fort Herkimer, 16, 17, 110; Fort Knyphausen, see Fort Washington; Fort Lyman, see Fort Edward; Fort Rensselaer, 16, 109; Fort Richepanse, see Fort Saint-Charles; Fort Saint-Charles, 68, 132; Fort Schuyler, 17, 110; Fort Stanwix, see Fort Schuyler; Fort Washing-

Forts (*cont.*)
ton, 8, 104; Fort William Henry, see Fort George
Foulquier, François de, 132
Foundries, 34, 46, 121, 124
Franklin, Benjamin, xi, xii, 39
Franklin, William, xi, 39
Fredericksburg, Va., 49
Free ports, 69
French Revolution, in Lombardy, xvi

Gambier, Adm. James, 76
Game, 101-2
Games, 21, 64
Gandolfi, banker, xi, xxiv, 57, 60, 100
Gansevoort, Leonard, Jr., 106
Gates, Gen. Horatio, 13
Gautier, Mr., 73
Gautier de la Rivière, François Jean Baptiste, 71
George and Cottin Company, 70
Georgetown, D.C., 47, 53
German Flats, 110
Giulini, Countess Anna dal Verme, xv
Glens Falls, 108
Gokley, Mr., 31
Gordon, Col. James, 15, 109
Graham, John, 49
Grand, Ferdinand, 97
Grand, Henry, banker, xi
Gray, Col. Neigal, 30
Grayson, Col. William, 49
Greene, William, 98
Greppi, Count, 81
Groton, Conn., 115
Grubb, Curtis, 34
Guadeloupe, 68-69, 133-34
Guana Island, 64, 131
Guerard, Benjamin, 54, 55
Guilford, Conn., 27

Haldimand, Gen. Frederick, 108
Halifax, N.C., 50, 127
Hall, George Abbott, 54, 56, 99, 128
Hamilton, Douglas, Duke of, xxii

142 Index

Hamilton, Mrs. Elizabeth Schuyler, 13, 106
Hammond, William, 46
Hancock, John, xxxii, 20, 23, 97
Hanover Court House, 49
Hansen, Miss, 50
Harrison, Benjamin, xxxii, 49, 98
Harrison, Peter, 115
Hartford, see Bel Air
Hartley, David, 97
Harvard College, 25
Hatch, Col. Lemuel, 50
Havana, 83, 85-86
Hawk, ship, 56, 60
Henry, William, 35, 121
Heriot, Col. Robert, 53
Herkimer, Gen. Nicholas, 110
Hessians, 38
High Rock Spring, 109
Hispaniola, 70
Hitchbourn, Benjamin, xxviii, 25, 114
Hooe, Col. Robert Townshend, 47, 49
Hoops, Robert, 50-51, 117
House, Mrs., 36, 37
Houses, transportation of, 45
Houses of worship: Middle States and New England, 22, 26, 29, 34, 112, 115, 121-22; Southern States, 55; West Indies, 68, 75-76, 86, 130-31, 132, 133, 134
Howard, Mr., 74
Howe, Lord Richard, xxi
Howe, Maj. Gen. Robert, 29, 117
Hudson River, 42; Palisades, xxix, 8; chain across, 11, 105; cataracts and petrifactions, 13
Hunter, Betsey, xxvii, 23, 25, 113
Hunter, Mrs. Deborah, xxxii, 114
Hunter, Nancy, 113
Hunter, Peggy, 113
Hunter family, 26
Hunting, 30-31, 51, 53, 54, 127
Huntington, Gen. Jedediah, 11
Hyrne, Maj. Edmund M., 55, 129

Indians, 13, 16-18; memorial of, 109; Oneidas, 107; Tuscaroras, 107; treatment of female captives, 107-8
Indigo, xxxi, 53, 58, 128
Interpreter, 66
Ipswich, Mass., 21
Iroquois, see Indians
Itineraries, xxviii
Izard, Ralph, 10, 55, 129

Jamaica, 73, 135, 136
James River, 50
Jefferson, Thomas, xvii-xviii; *Notes on the State of Virginia*, xviii, xxix, 99
Jenifer, Daniel of St. Thomas, 46
Jesuits, 47, 125
Jocelyn, Robert, Earl of Roden, xxii
Johnson, Sir William, 108, 109, 110
Jones, Willie, 50
Journal Américain, 136
Journal of the Antilles, 76

Kageneck, Count Friedrich, xii, 97
Kempenfelt, Rear Adm. Richard, 100
Killingworth, Conn., 27
Kinderhook, N.Y., 12, 19
Kingsbridge, 7, 8, 28, 103, 104
Kingston, Jamaica, 75
Klemm, John, 118
Knolton, William Peter, 118
Knox, Gen. Henry, 11, 92, 105

Laborde, François Louis Joseph de, 71
Laborde, Jean Joseph, Marquis de, 134
Laborde de Marcheville, François Louis Joseph de, 134
Lac St. Sacrament, see Lake George
La Fansette, ship, 71
La Grange, 71
Lake, Richard, 75
Lake Champlain, xvii, 14
Lake George, 13, 14, 108
Lake Oneida, 17, 110

Index

Lamberton, N.J., 47
Lamfrey, Mr., 26
Lancaster, Pa., 34-35
Langdon, Elizabeth (Mrs. John), xxvii, 22, 112
Langdon, John, xxxii, 22, 98
Laurens, Henry, xi, 39
Lee, Thomas Sim, 47, 125
Lehigh River, 30
Létombe, Sieur Philip Joseph de, 20, 21, 23, 24, 25, 26, 27, 91, 92, 113-14, 116
Letout, Mr., 73
Lewis, Col. Morgan, 19
Lexington, Mass., xxxi
Lillington, Gen. John Alexander, 51, 127
Lincoln, Benjamin, 97
Lititz, Pa., 34, 121; *see also* Moravians
Litta, Alberto, 11, 42, 44
Litta, Countess Amelia, xix, 99
Litta, Pompeo, xv
Livingston, John, 24
Lloyd, Dr. James, xxxii, 23, 24-25, 46, 47
Lodi, xviii
Logan, lament of, xxix
Logs, 5-6, 62
Lothian, William John, Marquess of, xxii
Loudon, *see* Otis
Loyalists, xxviii, 8, 27, 38, 43, 44-45
Luzerne, Anne-César, Chevalier de la, 29, 35, 116, 122
Lyme, Conn., 27

McLaine, Archibald, 51
Macnémara, Henri-Pantaléon, Comte de, 71, 134
Magnifique, ship, 113
Mail service, xxxii-xxxiii, 40
Maneuvers, 67-68, 132
Manheim, Pa., 34
Marblehead, Mass., 21
Marie Galante, 68
Markets, 64, 69, 130, 133
Marlboro, Mass., 19

Martha Brae, 73-74, 135
Martinique, 69, 70, 133-34
Mecarti, Capt., 74
Meetinghouses, *see* Houses of worship
Mercy-Argenteau, Count Florimond-Claude, xxi
Middleton, Arthur, 102
Miller, Rev. John Peter, 34, 120-21
Mills, 70, 133-34
Mineral Springs, 15, 109
Mines, 34, 46, 50, 121, 126
Mohawk River, 13, 17
Molliere, Mr., 23, 113
Mona, 71
Monica, 72
Mont Grand Diable, 75
Montserrat, 70
Moravians, xxx-xxxi, 31-34, 118-19
Morelli, Sigr., 85
Morris, Gouverneur, xxxii, 93
Morris, Robert, xxxii, 29, 35, 36, 37, 116
Morven, 105
Mosquitoes, 14, 108
Moultrie, Gen. William, xxxii, 54
Mount Diablo, 135
Mount Vernon, xxx, 49
Mühlenberg, Rev. Gotthilf Henry Ernest, 35, 121-22
Munford, Mrs., 76
Museums, xxx, 36, 102, 122, 123
Music, 31, 32, 33, 55, 56
Mutiny, Pa. troops, 7, 29, 39-40, 104, 116-17
Mystic River, 21

Nassau Hall, 10, 105
Natural Bridge, xxix
Nazareth, Pa., 31, 117, 118; *see also* Moravians
Negroes, xxviii, 47, 50, 52, 58, 64, 66, 125, 132, 136; punishment of, 68, 131; dances, 69, 133; dress, 69; diet, 131
Nelson, Thomas, 98
Neuville, Baroness Hyde de, 111
Nevis, 70
Newburgh, N.Y., 11-12, 106

Newbury, Mass., 21, 22
New London, Conn., 26, 115
Newport, R.I., 26, 115
Newspapers, 121
New York City, 7-8, 38-39, 40, 103-4
Niagara Falls, xxix, 101
Nicholson, Sir Francis, 124
Nicolau, Mr., 73
North Carolina, xxviii

Occoquan Creek, 49
O'Connor, Hugh, 75
Oneidas, see Indians
Opera, see Theatres
Opossum, xxix, 46, 101
Ordinaries, see Taverns
Organs, 31, 34, 118, 121-22, 130-31
Otis, Mass., 19
Otsego Lake, 17
Otto, Dr. John Matthew, 118

Paca, William, 98
Pagliacci, xvi
Palmer, Mass., 19
Parham, 63, 64, 131
Parsom, Mr., 69
Passaic Falls, see Totowa Falls
Passaic River, 10
Pavoy, Mr., 73
Peale, Charles Willson, xxx, 36, 117, 122
Petersburg, Va., 50
Petrarch, xiii
Pheasants, 31
Philadelphia, xxx
Pinnock, James, 76
Pocahontas, xxix
Pontew, Mr., 63
Porkins, Capt. John, 76, 136
Portsmouth, N.H., 21-22
Potatoes, 53
Potomac River and Falls, xxix, 47, 49, 126
Pownall, Thomas, 107
Prevost, Maj. Gen. Augustine, xxii
Prices, 43, 51-52

Princeton, N.J., 10, 28, 30, 36, 39-40, 105
Prisons, 29, 116
Providence, R.I., 25
Public functions, 63
Puccini, Giacomo, xvi
Puerto Rico, 70

Quakers, xxx, 29, 135

Raccoon, xxix
Racing, 22, 50, 127
Rainsford Island, 23, 113
Ramsay, David, *History of the Revolution of South-Carolina,* xviii, 99
Randolph, Edmund, 49, 50
Rappahannock River, 49
Read, Jacob, 10
Reading, Pa., 32-33
Red House, 108
Regina Indiana, ship, 73
Rhode Island, 26
Rice, xxxi, 53, 58, 128
Richmond, Va., 49-50
Rio Bueno, 75, 135
Rittenhouse, David, orrery, 10, 105
Roads: Southern States, xxviii, 46, 47, 51, 52, 53, 57, 101; Middle States and New England, 15, 16, 19, 20, 26, 28, 31, 35, 40, 109; West Indies, 74, 75, 127, 135, 136
Roanoke River, 50
Rocky Hill, N.J., 28, 30
Roebuck, ship, xi, xxv, 7, 8
Rogers, Col. Nicholas, 46
Rolfe, John, xxix
Roll, Sigr., see John Rolfe
Ronan, Ann, 64
Ronan, Margaret, 64
Rose, John, 64
Roseau, 69, 132
Roxbury, Mass., xxxi
Royal George, ship, xxi, 100
Rubens, Peter Paul, *Daniel in the Lions' Den,* xxii, 100
Rutledge, Edward, xix, xxxii, 54, 55

Rutledge, John, xix, 128
Rutledge, John, Jr., xviii-xix, 99-100

St. Ann's Bay, 75
St. Croix, 70
St. John's, Antigua, 63, 64, 66, 131-32
St. Leger, Col. Barry, 110
Saint-Pierre, 69, 70, 133
Salem, Mass., 21, 22
Santo Domingo, 71
Saratoga, N.Y., 13, 15, 107, 108
Saulais, Beaumé de, 132
Scala, La, xv, xix, 100
Schenectady, N.Y., 18
Schoepf, Dr. Johann David, xxvi
Schuyler, Abram, 106
Schuyler, Gen. Philip, xxxii, 13, 19, 106, 107; home at Albany, 12-13
Schuylkill River, 32
Scott, Alexander, 63
Sears, Isaac, 23, 25
Seed, 93
Seventh Day Baptists, see Dunkers
Sforza, Chiara, xiv
Sforza, Ludovico, "Il Moro," xiv
Sharks, 66
Sheafe, Miss, 92
Sheafe, James, 22
Sherman, Cornelius, 64
Shippen, Thomas Lee, xviii-xix, 99-100
Shirley, Thomas, 63, 130
Simitière, Pierre Eugène du, xxx, 36
Slavery, xxviii
Smith, Mr., 30, 49, 63, 66
Smith, Mr. (of St. John's), 63, 64
Smith, Abiel, 21, 25
Smith, John, xxix
Snakes, xxix, xxxii, 14, 102
Soulès, François, *Histoire des troubles de l'Amérique anglaise*, xviii, 99
South Carolina, 53
Spanish Town, Jamaica, 75, 135
Spotswood, Gen. Alexander, 49
Springfield, Mass., 19, 111

Staats, Gerrit, 106
Stagecoaches, see Carriages
Stamford, Conn., 27
Staten Island, 38
Steuben, Baron Frederick, 11, 14, 29, 108
Steward, Mr., 7-8, 11, 28, 39, 103
Stewart, Mrs., 35
Stiles, Rev. Ezra, xvii, 27, 115-16; letter from, 91
Stone, Mrs., 47
Sullivan, James, 23
Sullivan, Gen. John, 98
Sunday laws, 19-20, 111-12
Susquehanna River, 17
Swan, James, 23, 92, 113
Swann, John, 51

Tannenberg, David, 118, 121
Tarboro, N.C., 50
Tate, William, see Mr. Fate
Taverna, Guiseppe, "Beppo," xvi, xxv
Taverns, 47, 52, 127; Balling's, 75; Barber's, 26; Coffee-Room, 54-56, 129; Fraunces', 103; Makensy's, 75; Marlboro House, 125; Menig's, 75; Rose Inn, 31, 117; Smith's, 130; Sun Inn, 31, 118; White's, 53-54; Vareen's, 52, 125
Tayler, John, 19
Taylor, Mrs., 46
Temple, Miss, 92
Ten Broeck, Abraham, 12, 106, 111
Thanksgiving services, 129
Theatres, 7, 40, 69, 71, 72, 83, 104, 134; Teatro Dal Verme, xvi; John Street Theatre, 104
Thomson, Archibald, 75
Ticonderoga, 14
Toscanini, Arturo, xvi
Totowa Falls, xxix, 105
Tracy, Nathaniel, 24, 25, 98, 111, 114
Traincho del Sela, see Trammel's Place, Turkey Island
Trammel's Place, 47

Transportation of houses, 26
Treaties, 43, 45, 110
Trenton, N.J., 28
Trumbull, Jonathan, 98
Tryon County, losses in, 111
Turkey Island, 47
Turnbull, Dr. Andrew, 54, 55, 128
Turnbull, Maria Gracia, 54, 128
Tuscaroras, see Indians

Upper Marlboro, Md., 47

Van Berckel, Peter John, 35, 36, 122
Vaughan, Samuel, xxxii, 37, 123
Verme, Count Antonio dal, xiv, xv, xxiii; *promemoria*, xx; has son's communications copied, xxxii; letters to, 38-45, 57-60, 77-79, 83-84
Verme, Bonaventura dal, xiii
Verme, Ercole, xiv
Verme, Francesco dal (d. 1578), xiv
Verme, Count Francesco dal: arrival in New York, xi, 7; letters of introduction, xi, xvi, 19, 30, 77, 97, 98, 106, 111, 125; family name and arms, xii; birth, xv; marriage, xv; political views, xvi; visits Washington, xvi-xvii, 11-12, 28, 30, 36; departure from home, xx; clothing, xx, xxv; visits France, xx-xxi; visits England, Scotland, Ireland, xxi-xxii; studies English, xxiii; travel funds and expenses, xxiv, xxv, 3-4, 81; servant, xxv; return to Italy, xxv-xxvi; journal, xxvi, xxxii-xxxiii, 43, 57, 60, 61, 77, 80, 83; logs, 5-6, 62, 123; tour with Washington, 12-19; horses, 19, 20, 30, 51, 52-53, 56; baggage, 28, 29, 42, 74, 93; journey to New York, 38; letters from, 38-45, 57, 61, 77-85; travel plans, 57-58, 60; diploma, 92, 116

Verme, Jacopo dal, xiii-xiv
Verme, Luchino dal, xiii
Verme, Luigi dal, xiv
Verme, Marcantonio dal, xiv
Verme, Countess Maria Camilla Taverna dal, xv
Verme, Nicola dal, xiii
Verme, Nicola dal, son, xiii
Verme, Pietro dal, xiii, xiv
Verme, Abbot Pietro dal, xiv
Verme, Taddeo dal, xiv
Verona, xiii
Vidua, Count Carlo, 101
Vieux Cap, 71
Vincendon, Sieurs, 136
Visconti, Gian Galeazzo, xiii
Visconti, Countess Margherita dal Verme, xv, xxii-xxiii, 28, 44, 60

Walker, Henry, 50
Walsh, Antoine Jean Baptiste, 72
Warner, Jonathan, 21, 112
Warren, R.I., 26
Washington, Gen. George: xi, xxv, xxvii, xxx, 11, 28, 30, 49, 109, 116, 117; letters of introduction, xvi, 19, 28, 30, 98, 111, 115; tour, xvii, xxvii, xxx, 12-19, 30, 42, 106; expenses on tour, 89-90; congratulatory address to, 111
Washington, George Augustine, 26, 102
Washington, Mrs. Martha, xxx, 49, 102
Weare, Meschech, 98
Weasels, 34
Webb, George, 49
Westfield, Mass., 19
West Indies, 77, 81; society, xxvii
Weston, Mass., 19
West Point, N.Y., 11
Wetmore, William, 22
Whipple, William, 22
Willett, Col. Marinus, 19, 109, 110
Williams, John, 51
Wilmington, N.C., 51
Winn, Mr., 74, 75, 135

Witherspoon, Rev. John, 30
Wood Creek, 110
Worcester, Mass., 19
Worington, Gen., *see* Huntington, Gen. Jedediah
Wrentham, Mass., 25

Yale College, xv, 27, 115-16; diploma from, 91, 92

Zachee Island, 134
Zinzendorf, Count Nicolaus Ludwig von, 32, 119

Seeing America and Its Great Men

was composed, printed, and bound by
Kingsport Press, Inc., Kingsport, Tennessee.
The types are Garamond and Italian Old Style,
and the paper is Warren's Olde Style.
Design is by Edward G. Foss.